I0605621

Mindful Meditations *for* Black Men

Restorative Practices to Soothe Mind, Body, and Spirit

Jor-El Caraballo, LMHC
Author of *Self-Care for Black Men*

ADAMS MEDIA
NEW YORK AMSTERDAM/ANTWERP LONDON TORONTO SYDNEY/MELBOURNE NEW DELHI

Adams Media
An Imprint of Simon & Schuster, LLC
100 Technology Center Drive
Stoughton, MA 02072

First Adams Media hardcover edition
January 2026

Interior design by Maya Caspi
Illustrations by Tess Armstrong

Manufactured in the United States of America

1 2025

Library of Congress Control Number: 2025947942

ISBN 978-1-5072-2425-0
ISBN 978-1-5072-2426-7 (ebook)

This book is intended as general information only and should not be used to diagnose or treat any health condition. In light of the complex, individual, and specific nature of health problems, this book is not intended to replace professional medical advice. The ideas, procedures, and suggestions in this book are intended to supplement, not replace, the advice of a trained medical professional. Consult your physician before adopting any of the suggestions in this book, as well as about any condition that may require diagnosis or medical attention. The author and publisher disclaim any liability arising directly or indirectly from the use of this book.

Dedication

For my first best friend, I carry you with me always.

Letter to the Reader

Welcome! It's nice to meet you here. That you're reading this means one important thing is true: You are ready to dig deeper into your rich inner life and take control of the health and happiness waiting there.

As a Black man and therapist, I aim to provide people with the resources they need to be their fullest selves. I want people to experience a life with less stress, better mental health, and an ability to have a relationship with themselves rooted in deep self-compassion. I specifically want Black men to experience this as we are often ignored in mental health and wellness spaces. This book will provide you with the space to be with yourself as you follow mindful meditation practices that offer insight, heal deeper wounds, and call in self-love.

I wasn't exposed to the concept of mindfulness myself until I was a student in college, and even then it didn't quite fit into my life's practice until a few years later when I read Eckhart Tolle's book *The Power of Now*. Tolle introduced the concept of mindfulness as a means of personal reflection, self-compassion, and growth. *The Power of Now* inspired me to learn about mindfulness meditation as not only a concept, but a self-reflective practice of present-centered awareness with my thoughts and actions. And as I read through the book, I found myself in deep connection to the words on the pages. I learned about the power of being aware of the present moment. I was also experiencing this lesson as I read each section and chapter. I discovered that in these moments of reflection, my mind quieted and I was able to focus on things I found more important than any insecurities or anxieties I had about my own life and future.

This is the wish I have for you as you continue through the following pages. I believe that the gifts that come with mindfulness are things that you should be given whenever you can. *Mindful Meditations for Black Men* is my offering for any Black man who is seeking refuge from any pain or discomfort. Here I offer acceptance of your full humanity. I hope these meditations encourage and uplift you, and give you space to discover the power of mindfulness.

Your brother in wellness,
Jor-El Caraballo

Contents

Part 2: Body 83

Part 3: Spirit 149

Introduction

Black men are worthy of living full, healthier, more joyful lives. And one of the most powerful tools you can use for achieving the life you deserve is mindfulness. Mindfulness is the practice of being in tune with where you are in this moment, as well as how you feel, in order to reduce stress, improve emotional regulation, and create space for self-compassion. It is about taking intentional care of yourself and uncovering the things that allow you to adapt and thrive in a world that tries to hold you back. But what does this personal care and growth look like? How do you use mindfulness to address your different mental, physical, and spiritual sore spots in an impactful way? How can you carve out the time for mindfulness in the face of daily microaggressions and oppression?

In *Mindful Meditations for Black Men*, you will find answers to these questions in the form of meditation. More than a way to relax after a long day or calm racing thoughts, meditation is a mindful exercise that encourages you to slow down, be truly present with yourself, and release the judgments so often directed at Black men. In these reflective meditations, you will connect with your mind, body, and soul in order to explore your deeper thoughts and emotions. Each of the seventy meditations in this book covers a topic that speaks to the experience of being a Black man and invites you to use mindfulness to find the healing, insight, and progress you seek. You will:

- Explore effective ways of dealing with heavy emotions like anger and shame.
- Reject the expectations and prejudices of the outer world that only serve to oppress your true self.

- Challenge your own self-criticism, internalized pressure, and self-limiting beliefs.
- Release the wounds that weigh on your mind, body, and spirit.
- Discover opportunities to connect with your community and the guidance it can provide.
- And more.

As you make your way through these meditations, you will unlock the wisdom that lies in your own being. You are a strong and capable Black man; mindful meditation is simply the guide that will help you in your path to better health and wellness.

How to Use This Book

In *Mindful Meditations for Black Men*, you will have the opportunity to create moments of intentional mindfulness through the practice of meditation. First, you will be introduced to one of three important aspects of your being: mind, body, or soul. You will learn about how this aspect is connected to and nourished by mindfulness of the present moment, and how meditation specifically will call in this introspection. Then, in the entries that follow, you will practice different meditations to help you focus on the present and address any emotional, physical, or spiritual obstacles you might be facing.

Each meditation begins with an introduction to the main theme of that meditation, followed by a meditational phrase that you are invited to read aloud or contemplate during the practice. Next, you will dig deeper into the meditation itself, uncovering how to integrate it into your routine and carry its messages with you as you move forward in your life. These meditations include:

- Silence the Inner Critic
- Meet Your Body with Gratitude
- Create Space for Joy As Resistance
- And more

These entries themselves are the practice of meditation. By reading them you are engaging in the practice of present-centered awareness and contemplation on their core concepts.

You are also creating space for more self-compassion and acceptance. Society can be harsh and unforgiving toward those it struggles to understand and accept. Mindful meditation offers Black men a means of non-judgmental self-reflection, where you can acknowledge your thoughts and emotions, and identify patterns that stand in the way of greater health. Moreover, mindfulness through meditative practices has been found to have tremendous wellness benefits. These kinds of practices help reduce symptoms of anxiety and depression, improve your ability to focus and concentrate, and help you better understand and manage your emotions.

This isn't the kind of book that you should speed through in one sitting; these entries are practices that you should savor and internalize. Approach each one by setting an intention of focus and presence. Create an environment that is conducive to that for you. Find spaces that feel safe and allow you to be comfortable. Ideally, you'd be able to practice without any visual or auditory stimulation and noise, but that is not always realistic. Do your best in creating an environment that is accessible and helpful for you.

You may decide to sit with one meditation daily or weekly, or maybe even visit with multiple whenever you have the time to devote to practice. You can practice these meditations while either sitting up or lying down. You can read the entries in order or skip around to ideas or themes that feel most relevant to you and your life right now. However, you may want to start with the initial entry, Start with Mindful Awareness, before diving into others, so it's easier to find your footing in the practice of mindfulness (especially if you're new to this kind of focused attention).

Know that each time you decide to practice meditation, you're investing in yourself in a profound way. Over time, you'll start to see how much easier it becomes to pay attention to your thoughts, feelings, and internal experience during this practice. Use the information and insights you gain while meditating to positively impact your life and mental health on a daily basis. And above all, enjoy.

PART 1

Mind

The mind is incredibly powerful. It is the driving force behind our thoughts and decisions in navigating life. It is one of the most important tools we have to process and find meaning in our experiences.

One of the reasons why mindfulness is such a powerful tool is that it helps us develop a conscious relationship with our mind. Every time we practice listening or tuning into the depth and complexity of the mind, we create opportunities to deepen the connection we have with ourselves. This is what it means to develop presence with the self. This certainly isn't the norm in modern life. We are challenged by the dedication and hard work that come with developing a connection with the self. Sometimes we are more comfortable with the *performance* of a connection with the self. This is, in part, why so many psychological terms have become popular online and in mainstream culture. While we sincerely approach these ideas with deep curiosity to understand our own experiences, we unfortunately often rely on sound bites and watered-down versions that are easy and accessible. However, just like mindfulness, finding connection to ourselves and personal meaning usually requires a consistent practice of quieting down, limiting judgment, and simply paying attention to anything that we can discover.

Part of the avoidance of doing the inner work is, for a lot of people, fear. You might fear your own mind. Or what you may find when you start to look inward and listen. It's normal to have these mental barriers as they are part of your psyche's natural defense systems against discomfort and pain. But when you don't allow connection and presence with these somewhat scary parts, you rob yourself of the opportunity to find healing and more peace.

In this part, you will reflect on the relationship you have with yourself. In these entries, you are encouraged to create space to look inward and practice more self-compassion with whatever you find. Additionally, the meditations here also invite you to try on new ways of thinking. The new perspectives you will find here invite you to reflect on self-limiting ideas and thoughts that may negatively impact your mental health. None of this work is ever easy, but with more practice in mindfulness and simply being with yourself, the easier it becomes to tolerate some of the discomfort that comes with meeting yourself in these quiet moments.

Start with Mindful Awareness

Mindful awareness is a gateway to deeper personal understanding. When you learn how to become attuned to your inner experience, you are better equipped to listen to your internal voice in any situation that requires your mindful awareness.

MEDITATION: MINDFUL AWARENESS HOLDS THE KEY TO MY DEEPER UNDERSTANDING AND SELF-ACCEPTANCE.

What does it mean to be mindful? To be mindful means to exist in connection with the present moment. It means to connect with a sense of self, and the body, to center your focus on the present moment, to the exclusion of other life circumstances that may otherwise be a part of your world. In this presence you are able to experience insight and inner peace.

To start a practice of mindful awareness, you can connect with your breath. While breathing is, for most of us, automatic and natural, mindful breathing is a method of bringing conscious awareness to your body. This intention invites internal reflection. You may start by taking a few moments to notice how you breathe. As you do, pay attention to what happens naturally without forcing change. Observe the rise and fall of your chest as you breathe in and out.

Notice how your breath moves your abdomen as your body naturally takes in the oxygen it needs. Observe the sensations within your body. Imagine that you're describing what each breath feels like in your own mind as if it's a completely new experience for you. Where is that breath moving through your body? And what sounds is your breath making right now?

Once you've settled into a natural rhythm of breathing and noticing, shift your focus to any thoughts that may be coming up for you. Take note of where your mind travels when you slow down and practice mindful awareness.

What kind of thoughts or feelings come up for you? Remember that mindful awareness isn't about judging or changing; it's about noticing your present experience. You are simply observing how your breath moves throughout your body, and any thoughts and feelings that may be coming up for you. These thoughts are always there, influencing you and your choices, whether you connect with them consciously or not.

For Black men in particular, there's often so much pressure in squeezing the most out of every moment and every opportunity, for efficiency's sake. In these moments, your brain focuses on what you're doing and not how you're experiencing life. Mindful awareness brings you back to the experience. In it you can find understanding of the impact. This brings clarity.

When you slow down and take in the world around you mindfully, you see it differently. Connecting with your breath and your body helps you be more fully aware. You *experience* the world around you, as a full being—not just a mind focusing on moving from one task to the next without interruption. And when you're in the space of mindful awareness there is ease and freedom within. The more opportunities you take to practice mindful awareness, the greater sense of peace and ease you'll find. Keep this sense of mindful awareness in mind as you practice the other meditations in this part.

Normalize and Face Fear

Fear is a normal human emotion. For men, especially Black men, fear is not something we usually allow ourselves to acknowledge or talk about with others. Yet, giving ourselves the permission to access our feelings, and learn more constructive ways to respond to them, can provide a great deal of relief and help us live with more intention.

MEDITATION: I ACCEPT THAT MY FEAR IS A NORMAL HUMAN EMOTION.

Fear is natural, and yet so many of us find it difficult to acknowledge fear as a valid emotion for which we are hardwired. Given the cultural conditioning we are subjected to, Black men are taught that manhood also means always feeling brave, especially in the face of fear. While strength and bravery are necessary to carry throughout this life, it should not be at the exclusion of honoring feelings that are a part of the natural human experience.

So often, men are taught that to be the best version of themselves they need to be the ultimate providers and protectors. With this comes an incredible amount of pressure and fear. And yet, avoiding acknowledgment of the fear and anxiety of not potentially living up to these high standards has become the norm. But when asked pointedly, and in safe company, many men will reflect on just how much pressure they face in their lives. They will then go on to describe their experience without naming their feelings as anxiety and fear. Black men do not need to avoid fear or anxiety to see themselves as strong and capable beings.

To find peace within yourself, it's imperative to create space for all your feelings. To do so means giving yourself the unconditional love you deserve. Accepting your feelings just as they are is also a way in which you honor the fullness of your humanity. It is not virtuous to not feel fear, despite what social stereotypes and expectations might suggest. Not feeling fearful at certain moments is impossible. Fear is encoded in your physiology and is not just reserved for life and death moments. Fear and anxiety are a part of daily life more than you may feel comfortable acknowledging.

The world in which we live presents many challenges for Black men, and they can cause a great deal of fear. On the more apparent side, as Black men we can acknowledge what happens in our bodies and our spirits when we're entering an interaction with police. There is often panic and fear due to the long history of hostile policing of Black folks. In less apparent ways, fear manifests when we're faced with harsh critiques from our bosses at work, or our partners who request more of us. Our fears about being terminated at work, or being left by our partners, or not being seen as good (or man) enough can weigh on our minds and spirits. Consciously ignoring these feelings only contributes to the pain and isolation we experience. It keeps us from being truly present, aligned, and vulnerable with those we seek the most communion with. When deeper access is closed off within yourself, it's next to impossible to have someone else show up for you in the ways you find most meaningful.

As scary as it may seem, allowing yourself to acknowledge your fear is an important step in finding relief and being present with yourself. This meditation is an invitation to give yourself that permission, without judgment, to say, "I'm afraid," and listen. Give yourself a moment to sit with this feeling, consider your life circumstances that contribute to this fear, and observe what happens in your body and what sensations color your experience. Then practice presence and give your mind the ability to consider what you might need to help you manage this fear from becoming completely overwhelming. Let your presence guide you in discovering how to embrace more courage, while still acknowledging that it's healthy and normal to feel fearful.

To find peace within yourself, it's imperative to create space for all your feelings. To do so means giving yourself the unconditional love you deserve.

Let Go of Scarcity and Embrace Abundance

As human beings we are always conscious of resources. What we have, and what we don't have, are important assessments for our individual and collective survival. These assessments have been particularly salient for Black men, who have had to fight for our most basic needs at various points throughout history. When we become aware of what we have, we also become acutely aware of what we need. But what happens when we continuously find ourselves in the space of wanting and needing? Through mindful meditation, we refocus on an honest assessment in the present and stave off anxiety about what we might lose or have yet to gain.

MEDITATION: I AM ENOUGH. I HAVE ENOUGH.

As living, breathing beings, we need resources to survive. We must also meet our basic needs to succeed and potentially thrive. These principles were lessons from the Blackfoot Nation, who are believed to have inspired psychologist Abraham Maslow's hierarchy of needs. Many of us have come to understand this basic premise, and why we have the kind of community programming and activism that helps people get the resources they need. When we have what we need, we are able to think clearly, succeed in education and work, and build a life that can sustain us. Most of us believe these truths. What we don't often reflect on, however, is how honest our present assessment of resources is, and the way in which future- or past-oriented thinking can keep us from acknowledging and appreciating what we have in the now.

Culture and society often dictate how we think about our finances and resources. In most modern cultures in highly developed nations, we've long abandoned focusing on meeting our needs and have become preoccupied with our wants. Commercials and influencer culture continue to remind us of all the things we "must" have to feel okay and secure with ourselves. And then we become reactionary, always striving for that promise of a more secure future self. Unfortunately, as you may be realizing yourself right now, that often puts you in the position of being disconnected from the present moment and what you have now. If you are fortunate enough to earn more and thus acquire more, you are likely to experience a cruel heartbreak when you realize that the yearning for more continues—despite arriving at a place of resources you had only dreamed of. And thus, the cycle of worry and anxiety continues.

Alternatively, if you've only known scarcity and poverty, seeking more may seem like the salvation from your financial strain and pain. For you, abundance may become a symbol for the freedom you anticipate from having more. Unfortunately, it's not at all uncommon for the fear of poverty to loom even if someday you achieve access to many more resources. The fear and anxiety of going back to a past in which you scraped to get by preoccupies your thoughts.

No matter what side of the fence your experience places you on, you likely find yourself continually racing toward the future, reliving the pain of your financial past, or somehow cycling between the extremes like some catastrophic pendulum never able to rest in what is here in the now. This is the mental trap of scarcity. Not only will it exacerbate worry, anxiety, and mental strain, but it may also be reinforcing long-standing messages you have about your own value and worth.

This meditation is your invitation to acknowledge the messaging that tells you that you need more and more in order to be happy and fulfilled. Exhale the thoughts that you must work toward the someday that you will find yourself at peace with what you have. The moment for that peace is also right now. If your basic needs are met, then this moment is your opportunity to release old messages and try new beliefs that help you embrace the abundance that you have right now. Instead of "I don't have enough. I am not enough. I need more. I need to be more," try reciting the new message of "I am enough. I have enough. I do not need to be more."

You are enough as you are. You have enough. You do not need to be more.

Find Peace in Solitude

The world is a busy place, and it demands your attention. From navigating the responsibilities of daily life, to spending time with others, to the time that your devices can steal from you unconsciously, it can be difficult to truly be with yourself. Many of us struggle to make the time to exist in communion with our deepest selves. Leaning into mindfulness can help you find peace in solitude.

MEDITATION: I AM THE MASTER OF MY FATE AND IN THIS MOMENT, I CHOOSE PEACE.

Black men aren't often taught how to be with themselves. This might be surprising to you if you often find yourself alone or feeling disconnected from others. Being alone, or simply existing with your own thoughts, isn't necessarily finding peace in solitude, because finding peace internally is a bigger challenge than most of us would like to admit.

When was the last time you were able to sit with yourself, in silence, and feel at peace? When you've made previous attempts, has it been difficult for you to not jump from thought to thought? Have you found yourself physically restless and struggling to sit still? If so, these are signs that you find it hard to be at peace within yourself. Perhaps today you can start to approach solitude as an opportunity for discovery rather than another space in life you try to avoid.

This starts with having compassion for a restless mind. You do not need to look down on yourself for feeling restless or being concerned about the next thing. These are common perspectives in modern society. Finding peace in solitude means giving yourself permission to be vulnerable and acknowledge these barriers with self-compassion.

In this moment you may be recognizing the anxieties and worries you carry with you daily. For many Black men there is the pressure to strive and be excellent, to acquire more to support and care for those closest to us. Perhaps you are reflecting on the next step in your career, or the project that awaits your excitement and expertise. You may be dealing with worries about your relationships or your living situation not quite being where you thought it would be at this point in your life. If the recognition of these challenges brings up pain and discomfort for you now, know that is okay and a helpful step in finding peace for yourself.

Peace isn't about ignoring all that may not feel right within your world. Peace is about developing, and practicing, deep compassion for yourself as you sit with the challenges as they are. You are not perfect, and neither is the life you live. And life need not be perfect for you to find moments of peace and relief.

This is the moment to breathe in with conscious awareness of these challenges. As you reach your next breath, imagine you are releasing the weight of these burdens. You accept that this moment, in your solitude, is for release. As you sit in this practice you may also come to realize that other thoughts that feel challenging for you come up too. They also deserve your acknowledgment and acceptance of their impact on your life. You can acknowledge their impact and practice acceptance rather than rejection. You do not manifest problems by acknowledging their existence. Instead, you give yourself peace in recognition that they are simply part of your existence. You are the master of your own fate. You choose what happens next, and in this moment you can choose peace.

Peace isn't about ignoring all that may not feel right within your world. Peace is about developing, and practicing, deep compassion for yourself as you sit with the challenges as they are.

Notice the Beauty in Small Things

Presence is the ability to exist in mindful awareness of the here and now. You can cultivate presence in your life by the continual practice of slowing down and noticing the world around you. In a world that so often highlights negativity, oppression, and injustice, learning to notice the beauty in small things offers Black men an opportunity to grow resilient no matter the circumstances.

MEDITATION: BEAUTY IS PRESENT ALL AROUND ME ONLY IF I MAKE SPACE TO NOTICE IT.

For many Black men, recognizing beauty has become a lost art. You may be well practiced in recognizing the beauty or allure of a potential romantic partner, but what if you could see even more beauty in the world? What if being able to see the world with fresh eyes could bring you more peace?

We're not often taught to explore the world methodically or slowly. In fact, the practice of intentionally noticing the world around us runs contrary to the capitalist system in which we are bred. In our current world, slowing down means failure, and laziness, especially for Black men. The stereotypes we carry around Blackness and around masculinity often create a need to overcompensate and stay busy. We do this to please others, and the parts of ourselves that we are insecure about.

As you run around in hyperproductivity, stuck in the rat race of proving your worth, you are missing out on the little reminders that this moment you're in right now is enough. And there is beauty in being enough. For example, if you keep moving through life quickly, it's hard to recognize the joy in your child's face as they look into yours. Not slowing down keeps you from bearing witness to the beauty and resilience of the earth, as it brings forth new life each spring as the flowers bloom. Plowing through life also makes it hard to recognize the moment your partner's shoulders relax with your gentle touch. These moments, and many others, represent the beauty that is all around you, should you take the moment to slow down and recognize it just as it is.

In this moment right now, there is beauty around you too. Maybe the beauty is in the words on this page that offer you a new perspective. Or it is the potted plant nearby purifying the air and giving you the oxygen you need. Beauty may even be in the effort of someone near you, who's working hard to provide for themselves or their family. There is so much beauty all around.

As a Black man, you may not have been taught to see beauty in a way other than the physical, but many things in this life represent the beauty of creation, motivation, and inspiration. This beauty is sustenance for a life when what is grim is often so present and visible. Stay in the practice of noticing the beauty all around you. Try not only looking with your eyes, but with your heart, and you'll find beauty in every space you inhabit.

Practice Self-Compassion

In our world it's normal to be our own worst critics. Entire industries are built on our difficulties in accepting ourselves. As they market their products and we spend our hard-earned money in the pursuit of perfection, we unintentionally release our power and agency to meet ourselves with more kindness and self-compassion.

MEDITATION: I GIVE MYSELF PERMISSION TO MEET MYSELF WITH LESS JUDGMENT AND MORE KINDNESS.

It's easy to internalize a harsh internal voice if you've also come up in a harsh, or even an emotionally muted, environment. Within Black families, we still have so much work to do to continue to unpack and unlearn strategies, such as numbness, that have provided for our survival. It's difficult to be present with your emotions when you're living in dire circumstances. Unfortunately, Black folks continue to face the realities of navigating discrimination, underemployment, higher than average incarceration, and a host of other determinants of health and well-being that continue to be targeted and underfunded. There is still so much collective work to do.

When you are in the space of survival, it's difficult to make space for your feelings. In those moments, feelings can seem almost trivial. And yet, this kind of minimization or invalidation can foster the creation of internal scripts that make you respond to your own emotional reactions, thoughts, or feelings with coldness and judgment. Learning to respond with more self-compassion requires an unlearning and an ongoing practice.

One way you can start to practice more self-compassion is by getting in touch with your internal voice. Your internal voice is somewhat of an internal narrator that monitors your thoughts, feelings, and reactions. He's the "voice" that makes you think, "That was so dumb. Why did you do that?" when you've made a mistake. Take a moment to sit in meditative reflection on a moment recently in which this internal narrator appeared in your life. Under what circumstances did he show up (what happened in your life at the time)? And how did he respond? As you start to reflect on this voice more, you may find that his perspective is harsher than you like or were even aware of.

Imagine now that there is another voice, or another benevolent part of you waiting in the background. This voice wants to honor your thoughts and feelings with a bit more compassion. He wants to respond to you as a wise male mentor, or a good friend, might. He seeks to strike the balance in honoring your desire for greatness or achievement, but without the judgment or coldness you may be used to. He wants to help relieve you of some of the pressures you face as a Black man in this world. He encourages you. What kind of words would he say? Is there a person, or character, that he'd try to emulate with his voice of reason? Listen to him offering you these affirmations of encouragement for you to repeat to yourself:

- I am not perfect, and I do not have to be perfect to be great.
- I release the pressure to always be strong in the face of challenge.
- I give myself permission to meet myself with less judgment and more kindness.

As you continue to move throughout your daily life, remember that when you practice self-compassion in this way, you are unlearning self-criticism and releasing old stories that have challenged your mental health. Neither inconsiderate nor overindulgent, self-compassion offers you presence with your full humanity.

This practice is your blueprint to practice self-compassion more in the future. When you find the judgmental voice come back (usually when you've made a mistake or experienced some other hardship), give yourself a moment to come back to this practice. Investigate the words this voice may be soiling your psyche with. Then invite in the new mentor, the new compassionate voice, to respond with more thoughtful presence and intention. Give yourself the permission to practice self-compassion however often you need it.

Weather an Emotional Storm

When you are faced with difficult circumstances, you can feel trapped as if in an overpowering storm. If you are used to avoiding or minimizing your emotions when an emotional upheaval arrives, facing reality can be devastating. Even further, you may begin to scold yourself for feeling those feelings. Learning to weather the emotional storm helps you fully realize what it means to exist alongside your pain without judgment.

MEDITATION: I'M LEARNING TO WEATHER THE EMOTIONAL STORMS IN MY LIFE WITH MORE GRACE.

Stoicism, a sort of emotional numbness, is an alluring prospect for us as Black men. It gives us somewhere to place our difficult thoughts and emotions. Stoicism provides us with a neat little container in which we can place our doubts, fears, and challenges, all the while reinforcing the brave and unaffected face we are told to put on for the world. This works, until it doesn't. At some point we may find that the storage of our emotional stuff has reached its capacity, and stoicism can no longer provide us with the protection and control we so desperately desire. It is in these moments that we are faced with an emotional storm that we are unprepared to navigate.

I grew up in a small town in North Carolina. When I was young, a tropical cyclone, Hurricane Hugo, reached winds up to around 150 miles per hour and, at the time, was one of the costliest storms on record. It destroyed my family home, and my family had to relocate as many of us in the area sought to rebound from the incredible wreckage. Living in the Carolinas means contending with the possibility of these kinds of storms, but who is ever truly prepared for this kind of devastation? We certainly weren't. It was one of my first introductions to what resilience looks like following tragedy.

When you live in an area prone to natural disaster, there are provisions you put in place. You build homes with certain materials and survey the land to ensure it's suitable for the kind of buildings that will ultimately rest upon it. When an acute storm approaches, you secure the necessary food and water and board windows or doors to help mitigate the damage. In a similar way, with your mental health, you can exercise, journal, meditate, and go to therapy to help you maintain a sense of wholeness and grounding to deal with everyday life. But then, every once in a while, you may experience a rare emotional challenge or tragedy that makes you realize you can never be fully prepared when a cyclone hits.

The judgment that many place on themselves, especially as men, for feeling impacted or even "out of control" in these moments is unreasonable and punitive. How might you have come to believe that you are somehow immune to being rocked by life's storms? How can you believe that argument that to be a strong man, you can never succumb to forces beyond your control? If you want to be healthy, you cannot.

To practice mindful acceptance around life's challenges means to acknowledge that sometimes you will experience storms that temporarily rock your internal world. To be present with your pain in these moments is to recognize that sometimes you are not able to respond with strength and absolute control in a situation.

This reflection offers a meditation on the reality of your suffering and your temporary defeat by forces outside of your control. This does not mean that you resign and stay down, but it recognizes that sometimes the healthiest action you can take to survive difficult moments is to hold yourself close, hunker down, and simply wait for the worst of the storm to pass. Once you are able, trust in your ability and get up again, resume control, and then rebuild. Every man needs the ability to recognize you cannot live up to the pressure to be strong and resilient at every moment. Some moments simply call for survival, and in this recognition, there is no defeat.

Every man needs the ability to recognize you cannot live up to the pressure to be strong and resilient at every moment. Some moments simply call for survival, and in this recognition, there is no defeat.

Express Anger Constructively

For Black men, anger is a familiar emotion. Most of us don't like to think of ourselves as categorically angry, and yet, there may be times in life when our temper is on a hair trigger, almost waiting for the next moment to explode. Learning how to hold your anger and understand its roots can help you move forward in life with less internal strife. This reflection is an opportunity to meet your anger mindfully.

MEDITATION: I CAN USE MY ANGER IN SERVICE OF TRUTH AND JUSTICE.

Anger is a difficult emotion for most people. And yet, as Black men it seemingly comes so naturally for us. Its existence reflects the reality of living in the world with the recognition of having to bear pain, challenge, and oppression that is not of our own creation, and at times, having to smile in the face of our oppressors for our own survival. This anger is valid.

In one recorded conversation between renowned creatives Nikki Giovanni and James Baldwin, Giovanni expresses that she shouldn't be subjected to that pain or negativity of a Black man she spends time with. Baldwin argues that existing within community provides a haven to be our truest selves, with guards down and permission to express our frustrations freely. Giovanni responds that the people closest to us also deserve the "performance" of the smile we sometimes put on for others. It's an evocative and challenging call to action to explore how you, and your feelings, manifest in daily life and where you place that energy.

If you do not pay attention to your anger and allow yourself to express the often more tender emotions underneath it like hurt, humiliation, and sadness, you risk the unconscious destruction of everything in your path. In the wake of ongoing injustices, it can feel natural to allow the flame of anger to destroy all things in its path. But this represents a deep misunderstanding of the truth about anger. While anger is about destruction, it is also about creation.

At times, farmers may burn the soil they farm. This burning is called agricultural burning. It is sometimes used to mark the end of one crop season and to prepare the soil for another. The fire helps rid the soil of debris that no longer serves the upcoming planting. The ashes can help remove the debris, changing its form into more easily repurposed ash to aid in future growth. While it's not a common technique these days, it serves as a reminder of the utility of fire. It destroys, but it can also lay the foundation for something new.

The same principle can apply to rage or anger. When controlled, the fire of your anger can be useful. Anger can help you fight injustice in the world. Your anger can be the fuel to address and resolve change, if wielded with intentionality and consideration.

"Anger" is not a dirty word. Your anger is valid and yet it doesn't represent the fullness of your emotional life. Therefore, it cannot serve as the weapon by which you address any situation in which you find yourself dissatisfied. Anger is a feeling and a meaningful internal experience as much as it is a tool to right a wrong. You have the power, and the choice, to use your anger in a way that helps you plant a life that meets your needs. Your anger is the power you have to use your voice for good, to advocate for your needs, and to build more intimacy when you're able to share it in close connections. Where there is an angry man, there is also hurt. Giving yourself the space and freedom to see anger as a tool to access even deeper feelings can give you the relief you are so desperately seeking. Do no harm and tell the truth. Tell your truth.

Learn to Prioritize Mental Health

Mental health is complex. It represents the various manifestations of our unique psychology and mental functioning. It is the combination of the thoughts, feelings, and reactions to our experiences that help make up who we are. On societal and cultural levels, "mental health" has become yet another keyword or idea subject to political propaganda, manipulation, and misinformation. You can take your power back and learn to prioritize mental health on your own terms.

MEDITATION: I AM LEARNING TO PRIORITIZE MY NEEDS ALONGSIDE THE NEEDS OF OTHERS.

Mental health is more than just the conditions that line the pages of textbooks and diagnostic manuals. It is the complex interplay of physiological, emotional, and mental factors that make up how we navigate the world around us. Unfortunately, for far too long, Black men have been manipulated into believing that mental health for us is only about the ability to exist in overproduction to provide for ourselves and our families and contribute to a system that benefits from our continual exhaustion and ignorance. Black men are the inheritors of an unfortunate legacy that demands our silence on mental health. For too long have we allowed ourselves to think of mental health as an other-community problem. All the while, we've witnessed fathers unable to be emotionally present for their children, mothers too strained and overwhelmed to properly love on their kids, and family and community members struggling with a range of issues that seem to have no salvation or recourse.

These stories do not have to continue to be your story. Your thoughts and feelings matter. It is critical for you to give yourself the permission and the space to take your mental health seriously. If you can make the time to listen in on yourself mindfully, you will learn with great clarity what in your life and heart deserves more of your energy and acceptance.

For Black men, it's often so hard to create the space for this kind of mindful listening in. It requires moments of silence and refuge to get away from the psychological noise and chatter from the outside world. There are, of course, the messages and demands of the larger society and capitalism, always pleading for your attention, focus, and labor. There are also the needs of your own family and loved ones who you want to show up for, even if you're not able to show up in the ways you most like to.

It may seem counterintuitive, but a large part of showing up lies in the ability for you to be present with yourself. When you are too busy attending to the outside pressures and the lives and needs of others, you ignore your own. What are your needs? What struggles are you facing in your mental processes? What makes your heart hurt that likely needs more support and acknowledgment? This meditation is your invitation to pause, reflect, and connect with yourself. What do you need?

Learning to prioritize your mental health will be an ongoing and intentional practice. Not only will you have to make the space and time in your day or week to be present with yourself, but you may also have to defend these small moments of mindfulness from others' demands and expectations. But it is worth it. When you make time to prioritize your mental health, and address all that's lingering inside, you give yourself the best chance of moving forward and living life with your best foot forward . . . and with a lot more inner peace.

Embrace the Full Spectrum of Your Emotions

When we practice mindful awareness, it provides a greater sense of self-awareness that can help us better understand ourselves and our emotions. When you allow yourself to be more in touch with your rich internal life, you reduce internal psychological tension and create opportunities for deeper social connection.

MEDITATION: I DESERVE THE RIGHT TO UNDERSTAND AND ACCEPT MY EMOTIONS.

As Black men, many of us are not taught how to be in touch with our emotions, let alone armed with the tools to develop language to share our deepest thoughts and feelings with those closest to us. The inability to speak to our emotions leaves us unable to adequately respond to the questions "What can I do to help you? What do you need?" This difficulty knowing our own emotions also stunts our ability to offer the kind of support and understanding others want from us when they're having a difficult time too. When we cultivate a practice of looking inward and developing language to translate our emotional selves, all those difficulties shrink tremendously.

The meditational practice of embracing the full spectrum of your emotions requires you to have some quiet time with yourself. Being able to sit and practice being with yourself, with no distractions, can help you better understand the fullness of your emotional experience. Once comfortable, take a moment to think of a recent experience in which you felt some sensation or feeling. It could have been in reaction to a fun or lighthearted moment, or something more challenging like dealing with a critique at work, or an argument between you and your partner. Call back to those sensations you experienced then. Did you start to sweat or feel tightness in your chest? Maybe you felt a pit in your stomach or an urge to get up and leave. Noticing these kinds of sensations helps invite presence. And when you allow yourself to notice, remember that mindfulness is about creating the capacity to connect to yourself in the moment, with no judgment, only compassion.

Once you've reconnected to that memory, use your imagination to envision that feeling has morphed into a physical shape or form. If you were to close your eyes and imagine you were in a blank white room with only this shape in front of you, what would this object look like? Would it be as tall as you? Could it be something you could hold, or would it overwhelm the space you share with it? You can envision its other qualities too. Is its texture smooth or rough? Shiny or more matte? And what is its color? Would it be a deep dark purple or a bright yellow, for example? These colors help symbolize the nature of your feelings connected with this experience. Colors are highly coded with our emotions (e.g., red can indicate passion or anger, etc.), and our own personal interpretations illuminate meaning. Finally, as you imagine this object, do you think it would be heavy or light? Would you be able to move it entirely by yourself or need help moving it to another place in the room?

This mindful practice is creating a symbol for the emotions related to your experience. This can be a helpful way to bring clarity so you can later respond to the question "How did it make you feel?" With a practice of imagining your emotions, you have more language to describe what they feel like: "I'm feeling this heavy, kind of dark feeling. It feels like it could overtake me at any moment." This kind of reflective process highlights that you already have some language to speak about and understand your emotions. Sometimes you may just need tools to help you decode and share yourself with more clarity.

This meditation is an exercise in imagination, and it could even be helpful to replicate by drawing this object on paper if that's helpful. Give yourself permission to come back to this practice routinely so you can cultivate the capacity to better understand and process whatever it is you're feeling at any time. Every Black man deserves the kind of clarity and self-compassion that can come from embracing the full spectrum of his emotions.

Every Black man deserves the kind of clarity and self-compassion that can come from embracing the full spectrum of his emotions.

Silence the Inner Critic

Who we are with ourselves, in our own minds, reveals the truest representation of our thoughts and feelings. As scary as it may be to acknowledge this truth, if you can choose to acknowledge the loud internal voice that shows up in self-criticism, you can begin the process of mindfully reclaiming what's yours and redesigning it to be all your own.

MEDITATION: I AM RELEASING SHAME AND SILENCING THE INNER CRITIC.

When it comes to understanding what happens in the deepest parts of our brains and hearts, Black men are often overlooked. The trend to ignore the depth and fullness of Black male humanity is so ubiquitous that it has also become internalized. That is, we ourselves have also come to believe that we are nothing but strength and resilience wrapped up in shades of brown skin tones. This only keeps us trapped in more mental anguish and pain. Black men are more than the stereotypes that we may even believe of ourselves. Black men are also encouraging, protective, and warm to those we love most.

Living in an environment that devalues your internal experience, or the thoughts and feelings about your own experiences, also ignores that impact of the world on you. The world emphasizes strength when we're challenged with vulnerability or helplessness and "pushing through" under the guise of resilience amid trauma. With these messages comes the message that your thoughts and feelings are unimportant. When you are continually force-fed this limiting narrative, you start to believe it. Unintentionally you deny your own humanity with self-critical thoughts about how you're not good enough, or man enough, to withstand the various daily injuries. How is it okay to believe such harmful thinking about oneself?

Your thoughts, of which you have thousands per day, impact your mental health and your sense of motivation. Unchecked self-critical thinking exacerbates anxiety and depression, squashing any energy or motivation you have to carry out your plans and ideals. This inner critic takes on the messages of the world, reinforcing the racist, limiting self-defeating beliefs of how fragile your ego and masculinity must be if you're struggling. But this inner critic is not destiny.

It is not your fate to relinquish control of mind to the ideas rooted in the desire to keep you from yourself. This is your opportunity to challenge this inner critic if you haven't already. He may not be of your own creation, but you are his master, and you can direct how he operates now and moving forward. Be mindful of how he shows up and sabotages you, particularly in moments of challenge or struggle. Practice reclaiming your voice and giving yourself the care and affirmation you deserve. Call on the phrase, "I am releasing shame and silencing the inner critic," when you need to meditate on your power in divesting from harmful stories that rob you of inner peace. In every moment, you have the choice to reclaim your power for a life filled with more self-compassion and acceptance.

Release Guilt Around Self-Care

These days most people have found some sort of method to embrace self-care. And still, it can be challenging to allow ourselves to honor our needs with less guilt. As we learn to create more space for ourselves in our lives, so must we learn to challenge the guilt that comes with prioritizing the self.

MEDITATION: I AM RELEASING GUILT AROUND TAKING THE TIME TO TAKE CARE OF ME.

Have there been times in your life when you made space for yourself, maybe some downtime, only to find your time and space challenged by someone else? Have you also found it difficult to settle into your self-care time, and struggled with restlessness or ruminating thoughts? If so, it's likely you've come face-to-face with some guilt around self-care.

Guilt is a natural human occurrence. At best, it is a part of the mind's makeup to help us engage in choices and actions that are aligned with our personal values. Often when we stray from those values, we get this nagging sensation that we've done something "wrong." This is what it means to feel guilty. Guilt can be easier to identify when you know you've done something wrong, like making an error at work or being caught in a lie. Guilt in these moments can make sense, especially if the transgression was an intentional choice. Then why would we struggle with guilt when it comes to practicing self-care?

Unfortunately, many Black men have not been taught to prioritize taking care of their mental health and overall wellness. Doing routine maintenance and practicing self-care, because of how we culturally define these ideas, have been linked with unmanly behavior. It hasn't been manly to see a doctor, seek out therapy, practice meditation, or reflect on our thoughts and feelings. As a result, these ideas cannot be aligned with how we like and sometimes need to see ourselves. These ideas around self-care aren't aligned with our values regarding manhood and masculinity.

What if you were able to redefine those values? Consider this meditation on guilt as an invitation to imagine self-care being a part of every man's duty and responsibility. If you're not well and actively maintaining yourself, how could you be the man your family or loved ones need you to be? How can you possibly be there for others when you're not even there for yourself?

This practice is an encouragement to meet yourself with more self-compassion and kindness when you need to take time for yourself. No matter how much you achieve, you will always need time for rest and self-care. When guilt comes knocking at the door to your mind, simply practice mindfully acknowledging it and refusing to let it in. Instead, make the choice to reframe your self-care as a part of your greater care ethic. When you are well, you are more empowered to show up in life, meet your goals, and take care of what's most important.

Believe In Your Ability to Achieve Your Dreams

How can one believe in the ability to achieve one's own hopes and dreams when there is so much external noise and so many barriers to being seen as equal and deserving? This question represents a critical inflection point in the lives of Black men as we contend with the themes of personal responsibility and the realities challenging communal success. Mindfulness provides for us a practice to quiet the noise and return to self-belief.

MEDITATION: NO MATTER WHAT CHALLENGES I'VE FACED, I ALLOW MYSELF TO DREAM AND START ANEW.

When I first came across Langston Hughes's poem "Harlem" (also known as "A Dream Deferred"), I was rattled. As a young Black boy, it was one of the first times I felt myself, and my struggles, reflected in literature. Hughes's poem explores how we move forward when our deepest hopes and dreams seemingly offer no possibility of coming true. It's a powerful reflection on the Black experience, particularly with its painful history in the West. While there is no easy answer to Hughes's question, we can be inspired to find refuge in the stories of resilience all around us.

As difficult as it may be to imagine a world in which your hopes and dreams come more easily, it's critical to look back at our collective history. Black folks have been resistant and resilient for millennia. That resistance is an exercise in faith and an ability to see beyond what is right in front of us. It's an acknowledgment that with every challenge, and every obstacle, part of our legacy as a community is our enduring spirit.

This awareness may be something that some carry with them consciously, but for most, the power of ancestorial legacy isn't something acknowledged on a day-to-day basis. Sometimes you may need a prompt, or a reminder to slow down, and contemplate collective inner strength. In these moments, the invitation is to continuously challenge defeating narratives and stereotypes from others who are not invested in your success.

Whether you like it or not, sometimes you may internalize these messages, and their impact can have devastating consequences. These mental consequences (frustration, low self-worth, etc.) can be especially damaging if triggered by some real-life event in which your ability to succeed or achieve has been called into question.

As you sit in this moment of reflection, what are the stories or messages that challenge your belief in your ability to achieve? Perhaps there are experiences you've had with educators, supervisors, or even family members who have told you that you can't possibly achieve what you set out to do. In this meditative moment, consider that you are more than those messages and harmful stories that have become part of your own internal voice over time. This is the moment to acknowledge them for the harmful tropes they are and release them. You can begin again, anew.

The resilience of your ancestors is within you and can be continuously cultivated to help you get closer to your hopes and dreams. You are more than your failures. You are also resilient and abundant. In this moment, you are coming home to yourself and embracing your ability to start again. Take this inspiration from your ancestors to adapt and dream once again.

The resilience is within you and can be continuously cultivated to help you get closer to your hopes and dreams. You are more than your failures. You are also resilient and abundant.

Move Forward Despite Uncertainty

Black men face the challenges of individual and structural oppression, discrimination, and the pressures to survive and somehow thrive despite that. In the hopes for a better future, one where our dreams of success and hopes for more ease reside, we charge forward. However, this doesn't mean that we can't create space to understand the journey in doing so and find refuge in conscious awareness of the toll that moving forward despite uncertainty requires.

MEDITATION: CERTAINTY IS NOT GUARANTEED IN THIS LIFE. AND YET, I PERSIST.

The human brain is brilliant in its complexity. It can inspire incredible creativity and efficiently help us navigate daily life with relatively little conscious effort, if we are so able-bodied and privileged. And yet, we may still experience a great deal of stress and anxiety as we try and move forward into the unknown. This is particularly true for Black men who are routinely told to keep our heads down and do the work, even when we are fatigued. We are continuously taught to move forward in the hopes that the future world around us will meet us with care and investment in our success. These steps forward, however, can feel so tiring when we don't know where exactly they lead.

You may have found yourself continuously frustrated, or even exhausted, at the continuous striving for more in a world where some are working to repeal progressive legislation that has helped Black folks rebuild, or acquire, resources that have long been due. At times you may find yourself feeling anxious and possibly even hopeless about the future that lies ahead.

To this I offer you this present moment for refuge. The breath that you hold within your body right now is part of the life force that energizes and sustains you. There is no progress, nor fortitude, without acknowledging the strength and resilience you already hold in your body and mind. You have already faced many challenges surrounding what is uncertain, and persevered. This is a moment in which you can breathe, allow your shoulders to drop, and honor all that it has taken for you to arrive here, brought together by the words on this page, to a present that was once a mystery.

The present moment is an opportunity for refuge. It is not only your breath that brings peace, but also the space your nervous system has right now to acknowledge and digest all your efforts to achieve a healthier, more humane future for you and your brothers and sisters out there who seek the same. Give yourself permission to be with this breath, and with this moment. Honor this moment and yourself, just as you would someone else who works hard bolstered by faith, with hope of the future realized in certainty and peace.

Overcome Impostor Syndrome

Impostor syndrome is a psychological phenomenon where you think you are not qualified for the position or role that you hold. For most people this manifests as anxiety in being "found out" as undeserving and losing your position or role. This often leads to feelings of unworthiness and worry over time, and can, unsurprisingly, lead to dysfunction and performance issues. In facing these challenges with mindful presence, you can begin to overcome them.

MEDITATION: I AM WORTHY OF EVERY SPACE AND OPPORTUNITY I ENCOUNTER.

The talk around impostor syndrome largely focuses most on those who suffer from it, rather than the people, and systems, that create it. This is of disservice to Black men. Black men do not naturally find themselves unsure of their abilities or potential in work or educational settings. More so, impostor syndrome is the conclusion of a lifetime of messaging of "You don't belong here. You're not good enough." We internalize these messages, even if we aren't entirely conscious of them. Impostor syndrome is insidious and can convince you that not only are you not able to do the work you set out to do, but you'll never be worthy of the positions you seek or find yourself in.

This set of beliefs is the enduring legacy of racism in action. Black men have historically been kept out of institutions of higher education, faced carceral punishment in school settings from a young age, and been forced into assimilation and code-switching for survival. Continuously feeling out of place, or unwanted, simply for existing as you are, is a special kind of suffering that no human being should have to experience. And yet, you endure. So too do women, LGBTQIA people, disabled folks, and other communities marginalized by the "isms" of society. Impostor syndrome is not a character flaw; it is the result of persistent and systematic messaging meant to demean and devalue your potential and abilities.

As you sit with this realization, this is your opportunity to release yourself from any responsibility for moments in which you felt you weren't good enough. Maybe there are circumstances in your life right now that make you feel this way. There may be bosses, or other folks in positions of authority, that demean or belittle you. This is not your burden to carry. As a Black man, you are not represented by the beliefs of those who continuously fear your success and improvement in society. These beliefs are nothing more than tools of oppression designed to make you doubt the greatness you have within you. As the next breath leaves your lungs, release those narratives and give them back to your oppressor. They are no longer yours to hold.

You are resourceful. You are resilient. You are worthy of every space and opportunity you encounter. Continue to remind yourself of these affirmations anytime you feel at odds or uncomfortable in these high-pressure environments, or when you're made to feel less than. That could not be further from the truth.

Impostor syndrome is not a character flaw; it is the result of persistent and systematic messaging meant to demean and devalue your potential and abilities.

Heal Financial Trauma

Who are you in the face of financial trauma and tragedy? Many of us have experienced periods of unstable income or poverty, or even unstable housing or homelessness. These hardships and trauma filter into our minds and personal stories for the rest of our lives, changing our relationship with financial resources. While these stories may continue to influence us, they do not have to be fatalistic. As you heal, you can become the architect and the author of your personal stories. Having the courage to face yourself, your stories, and your pain is the critical place to begin healing.

MEDITATION: MY FINANCIAL PAST DOES NOT DEFINE ME. I AM THE ARCHITECT OF MY FUTURE.

When was the first time you became aware of what money was? Most of us have stories about being handed money by our parents to get snacks or candy from a neighborhood store. For some of us that was a regular occurrence, and for others, this kind of moment was an unexpected treat. Which story was true for you, and how did that make you feel then? What about now?

This simple reflection provides you a window to begin exploring the role of money and finances in your life. Within these kinds of stories, you most likely have some experiences that led to increased awareness, or even stress and anxiety, about what it meant to have money, and conversely what it meant to not have enough of it. Unfortunately, one part of many of our stories as Black folks is a reflection on hardship and trauma. In the United States in particular, we have yet to be able to fully realize the dreams of our country's foreparents, but not for the sake of not trying.

Discrimination and other obstacles have plagued Black folks and our plans for financial success for hundreds of years, to the present day. Some of us have been able to find a modicum of success and intergenerational wealth to pass on to our children. Yet there is still so much ground to cover as we've yet to see reparations for all the money and labor oppressors have stolen from our ancestors, alongside the erasure of our ancestors' culture, contributions, and history. But no matter where you are in your life right now, please recognize there should be no shame in your struggle.

While the financial trauma of Blackness comes with this legacy of dehumanization and theft, you also must contend with the individual experiences you've manifested in your life with money, or the experiences that may have rocked your sense of security in your family of origin. Layoffs from jobs, moments struggling to pay for groceries at the market, and cards declining at the gas station add to the shame and guilt experienced in traumatic financial times. But you have the awareness and insight now to take further steps to set up a better financial future. This process begins with mindfulness.

This is the moment that you can start to heal from those financial traumas you may have faced in your own life. The stories of your ancestors long ago, and the stories from your own life that may be springing up to consciousness now, are part of your story, but not the entirety of it. As you sit in reflection in this practice now, you can give yourself the opportunity for self-compassion for any trials or mistakes you've faced. You are not your hardships, nor are you destined to repeat stories of financial struggle and trauma. Your histories are not deterministic, only informative.

As you continue to reflect on the financial traumas you've faced in your life so far, try to look at them with fresh eyes. How can you see this moment as an opportunity to take control of your story from here on out? With this new perspective and opportunity, consider not only the pain that comes with your history, but what lessons and teachings you can take from what you've experienced. Let the past inform the reflections of now and inform your future. Give yourself the grace that you deserve. And remember, you are the architect of your future. Now is the time to build it.

Face Financial Fears and Cultivate a Healthy Mindset

Financial stress is one of the biggest contributors to the mental health and wellness of any person in modern society. As we center a sense of self, and our work, on our connection to money, we end up prioritizing it. And when we prioritize money, it becomes the center of our world. Preoccupation with money (getting it, keeping it, and spending it, etc.) drives our behavior and exacerbates any existing narratives we have about our finances.

MEDITATION: MY NET WORTH DOES NOT DEFINE ME AS A MAN.

Many of us have financial issues. In a society driven by what we own, money is an obsession. Even our dreams and quiet moments can revolve around how we acquire more wealth. In this kind of society, money symbolizes freedom and liberation, but it is nothing of the sort. This preoccupation can wreak havoc on our minds and sense of peace. To be preoccupied with money and with finances means striving further away from deep meaning within ourselves and what truly matters. We end up losing focus on what brings us happiness and promotes true well-being.

This disconnection with the self places all of us in the position to not be in the here and now. And when we are not in the here and now, we are either searching for a future not yet materialized, or healing from a past that still burdens our minds and our attempts at finding peace. This inherited legacy often operates in the mind of Black men unconsciously and drives a desire to overcompensate and be hyperproductive that negatively impacts our health and wellness.

When our ancestors were stripped of their humanity and enslaved, they became workers and cattle for white enslavers. This forced servitude enabled white folks to gain the wealth that our ancestors never got to realize for themselves. Not many Black folks in the world today have been able to reach the level of intergenerational wealth of even the white people back then, let alone now. And when Black folks did find success in history, their dreams were destroyed, like with the war and destruction in Tulsa, Oklahoma, in 1921.

We carry this legacy of financial worry and fear within us now. It is in the stories of our childhoods when parents struggled to make ends meet and encouraged us to be perfect and hyperproductive to achieve even more than they were able to provide. This has reinforced the pressure and preoccupation we face in the world at large, creating a sense of restlessness and unease with finances that plagues us. This pressure can be particularly damning for Black men, as we carry with us the gendered expectation of success being manifested as financial acquisition and wealth.

But you are more than your bank accounts, more than what you can acquire. You are a being full of a legacy and wealth that cannot be measured by a stock market or account number. You are more than what, and how much, you make.

Striving for more is your decision and your right, and this meditation is an invitation to challenge yourself to acknowledge and hold the financial fears and worries that have woven their way in your life and psyche. This is the moment to ask yourself, "As I think about money and success, what fears or worries influence my decisions? And how do those worries challenge my overall well-being?" Consider how you can move forward with money not from a place of fear, but from a place of wholeness and balance.

Never forget that your life is worth so much more than a calculation of net worth. Give yourself a moment to reflect on what truly makes up your value (your character, ethics, and morals), take a deep breath, and move forward with more insight and intention with money. With this new direction, you will gain more presence and ease in each moment, because in the here and now, there is less room for worry—only space to acknowledge what is and a breath that brings you ease.

Never forget that your life is worth so much more than a calculation of net worth.

Decrease Stigma in Your Community

Just like nature, human beings also experience growth and strength, erosion and weakness. The cycles of birth and death, rest and rejuvenation are part of our biological makeup, and yet we often fight what is natural. With one comes the other. Armed with acceptance we can find the courage to honor our struggles and fellowship with others who are also on the same complex journey of life.

MEDITATION: I AM MAKING SPACE FOR MY STRUGGLES, AND IN DOING SO I GIVE MY BROTHERS THE SPACE TO DO THE SAME.

"Stigma" is a word that gets thrown around often, but what does the word mean for Black men and the community at large? When it comes to the mind, stigma means a few things, most notably the difficulty we face as a community in addressing mental health. As of 2025, suicide is one of the leading causes of death for Black people aged 15 to 24. This is a mental health crisis that you probably haven't heard much of, and this is likely due to the stigma that we, as Black men, attach to struggling with our mental health. Admitting that you're in the depths of depression or struggling to find a way out of constant anger or irritability is difficult. It's never easy, particularly for Black men, to say, "I need help."

Born out of a righteous and divine need for survival, we've unintentionally created a trope around Black men's mental health that has become a prison. We cannot acknowledge even to ourselves how much we struggle, lest we face the agony of shame that washes over us for not being able to harness the strength of our ancestors who seemed to deal with so much worse. The never-ending focus on feeling strong and independent is not a hero's journey; it is a fool's errand. We all experience seasons in life that may be more challenging than others, much like the harsh notes of winter where the lack of sunlight so often mirrors our misery. We all have times in which we need help to recover and find inspiration that there is something beyond the darkness and pain that we are currently experiencing. Much like nature's cycle, a new season is always on its way.

Being a Black man doesn't mean you're invincible in the face of trauma and pain. These moments of personal challenge are just as much a part of life as are the moments of achievement and joy. You are not able to experience the heights of one without the depths of the other. This is the natural order that deserves your radical acceptance. Decreasing stigma within the community means adjusting your mind and allowing yourself, and others, to experience your full humanity, darkness and all.

In moments of pain, allow the presence of pain without judgment. Decreasing stigma starts with your mindful acceptance right now. This pain may also be something you remember from a time in the distant past when you weren't protected or cared for in the ways that were necessary. To be a Black man who challenges stigma, in this moment, is to accept what is.

You do not manufacture pain or manifest pain as a matter of choice. Challenge simply arrives. You experience it and it's valid that you do. Giving yourself the space to be with your pain gives you the ability to hold your brothers' pain in a moment when they may also need it the most.

Allow the pain. Give yourself permission to acknowledge and honor it. Offer the space for those around you to share theirs with you, and in each moment you do so you chip away at the internalized voice that makes you recoil from moments of weakness. That vulnerability, that pain and struggle, is one part of you, and it needs attention too.

Heal Through Collective Experiences

One of the greatest lies that we've been told is that we must, and are able, to make it through this world on our own. In the Western world there is a lot of emphasis on singularity and on the ability to thrive on your own accord. Thankfully, the adage of "pull yourself up by your bootstraps" is slowly falling out of favor. We must continue to forge ahead and challenge the notion that there is any chance of success that is not collective.

MEDITATION: I DO NOT CARRY THE WEIGHT OF THIS WORLD ALONE.

The modern world thrives on separateness and competition. These values are rooted in the globalization of capitalism, and we've been force-fed their importance for many years now. These values are the same ones that exacerbate internalized messages that tell Black men that to be of any real value to the world, and to a potential partner or your family, is to outearn the next man. The tides of patriarchy and whiteness continue to pull at the threads that bind us in solidarity.

This pressure is the same idea that challenges your ability to allow yourself the beauty of healing in connection with others. You may desire to be fully seen for who you are, and what you are challenged by, but are afraid for what it means to be really seen and supported, particularly from another man. But what this perspective fails to realize is that we share roots with others across families and times. Their stories are our stories. And in those connections are stories of not only struggle, but resilience, inspiration, and hope. You deserve to bear witness to them all. These stories and perspectives, which are only shared in the most intimate of spaces, are available to you only if you dare to be vulnerable enough to request them.

Being a Black man in this world does not mean that you are to shoulder the suffering of life alone. In the halls of churches, in community spaces, in sports halls, and in homes over shared dishes and bottles, there is room to share the burdens of life. In therapy offices and virtual rooms, there is healing that can only be achieved through the courage to share and hear one another with open eyes and hearts.

Healing within community is a brave and necessary act. As fascism and racism continue to dominate modern thought, there are opportunities to help you wield the weight of life alongside others. No one in the world is truly alone, despite the difficult times in which you may think that you are. In every moment that you feel the pangs of that isolation rise to the surface, remind yourself of those roots that ultimately do connect you with your community. Leverage the access you have to your brotherhood. In these more challenging moments, take in a full breath and remember that you are not alone. Remember that in the next room, the next home, the next healing space, there is connection and healing. You do not make your way through this life alone. Allow yourself to hold on to the healing that community has for you.

Give Yourself Permission to Learn and Release Shame

As people, we are often our own worst critics. We may hold ourselves to unrealistic high standards even without acquiring the knowledge or skills to reach a goal we have in mind. And then we may feel guilt and shame for our perceived failures, despite not being set up for success in the first place. For the sake of our mental health, we must develop a practice of giving ourselves grace and grow more comfortable with the humility and vulnerability of not knowing. This is an invitation for you to begin to do both.

MEDITATION: WITH EACH BREATH, I GIVE MYSELF PERMISSION TO LEARN AND GROW.

Pressure. It's a feeling that so many Black men are intimately familiar with, yet we don't often have the words to describe the burning sensation that rages within our chests when we are supposed to be reaching some new goal or achievement. And yet somehow, this pressure is always there, creating a sense of worry and anxiety that somehow always blares inside our spirit. Paradoxically, this worry is so ubiquitous and never-ending, it simultaneously and magically fades into the background at times, much like the sounds of nature do when we spend a bit more time in it. We get used to the pressure without ever having made a conscious decision to do so. But this anxiety is not only the rustling of the leaves of the trees in the background, but it is also the sirens of ambulances veering toward an emergency. It's time we start to take its warnings seriously.

For many of us, formal education was touted as a way to progress in our lives. Throughout the African Diaspora, this manifests in different sayings or customs, but I've yet to meet a Black person who was afforded the privilege to experience education without the awareness that not only were they doing it for themselves but also for their families, and their people who fought, often to their own peril, to attend school or let alone learn how to read. And so the stories we inherit often manifest as a lot of pressure not only to be educated but to always be learning and growing. We grow up believing that we must know everything to become successful. This kind of perspective can motivate, but it can also foster the development of a level of self-criticism and internal pressure leading to an ever-present anxiety about the future we have yet to realize.

But human beings cannot be all-knowing and perfect. Not every Black man can live up to such standards all the time. As you sit here with these ideas, try to internalize the following words and give them the power of your presence.

It is impossible to go throughout life having all the answers and doing everything perfectly all the time. For Black men, this has brought us to the precipice of perfectionism. Black men don't identify with this term often, but when faced with criticism or some sense of perceived failure, we become angry, irritable, and defensive. This is because in these moments you see yourself through harshness. You internally judge and berate yourself for not living up to the well-informed, infallible man you were told you had to be to be of any value. Ignorance, or some perceived failure, activates the ugly shadow of shame that you believe that overachievement and hyperproductivity will save you from. The harsh reality is that they will not. You must begin to save yourself with self-compassion.

Take a few deep breaths now and open your consciousness to a more compassionate and realistic perspective. You are not perfect, and you don't have to be. You don't need to feel shame for the things you have yet to learn. This is the moment in which you can start to give yourself grace as you grow and learn. The sense of dread you may feel when you lack knowledge is not of your own creation, yet it is your responsibility to practice releasing now. You have permission to learn and grow. You are not defined by your mistakes. You are not your shame. Repeat these notes back to yourself when you struggle with the shame of not knowing.

You have permission to learn and grow. You are not defined by your mistakes. You are not your shame.

Release Mistakes

It's easy to be hard on ourselves. There is an ongoing pressure to perform and live up to society's unrealistic standards. This is especially true for Black men. The pressure to perform and be a certain kind of Black man to be successful is an ongoing burden that can seem impossible to release. But, for the sake of your mental health, it's important to try to release external pressures you may have internalized to be and do all things perfectly.

MEDITATION: MAKING MISTAKES DOESN'T MAKE ME A BAD PERSON; IT MAKES ME HUMAN.

Black men often forget that we are, first, human. You have access to every feeling and thought that any other human being can experience. Your burden may be the pressure to be perfect, but you are more than the pressure you face. The pressure to be a perfect representative of your culture and never make mistakes is not reasonable, nor is it a healthy foundation upon which you build your mental health. It's healthy to acknowledge this pressure exists and has an impact. This moment offers you the space to acknowledge and meditate on releasing it.

Challenges you face in your daily life impact you the same as they would anyone else. Sometimes that means you might lose focus and make a miscalculation or mistake. Black men are entitled to make mistakes. You can forgive yourself for moments in which you're not the picture of perfection.

Take this moment to give yourself permission to release the burden of perfection. From your parents to work colleagues to teachers, professors, and maybe even your romantic partner, this is a time to acknowledge your right to imperfection as a human being. No one else has the right to dictate what you think or feel about yourself. This moment is for you to craft a more humane internal narrative. *You* are now the author of your own story.

Take a deep breath in and read these self-affirming statements aloud:

- I am a human being, and I am allowed to make mistakes.
- I can learn and grow from my mistakes.
- I am not meant to be perfect.

Carry these affirmations with you as you move through your day mindfully. Embrace the value of making mistakes. It's okay to make them. And from these mistakes, you learn. You learn how to soften your tone in a moment of conflict or how to take more time to weigh large life decisions with better judgment moving forward.

Mistakes are a normal and healthy part of living. You are not meant to be perfect to be loved. You do not have to be perfect to be valued and worthy. You are forgivable. You do not always have to chase excellence or perfection. You can give yourself permission to be just as you are right here and right now.

Build Connections with Other Black Men

Humans are interdependent creatures. Not only do we need each other for survival, but social and community connections are also healing for us. Each moment we spend connected to another is an opportunity to see and be seen, to mirror and be mirrored, to hold and be held. As the often cited, yet uncredited, proverb says, "If you want to go fast, go alone. If you want to go far, go together."

MEDITATION: I GIVE MYSELF PERMISSION TO SEE AND BE A MIRROR TO BROTHERS AROUND ME.

You may not realize it, but one message that many of us get growing up as Black men is that our lives are our independent responsibility. That is, in order to be considered "real" men, we grow, achieve, and profit from our own making. We get the message that to survive and thrive, we must forge ahead with all the strength and might we can muster, consequences and connections be damned. In its inception, this kind of messaging was born out of a desire to help us create lives that are generous and worth living—lives without the harshness and struggle that our ancestors faced. But without challenging the limitations of this messaging for us, we can easily find ourselves swimming in its liabilities, wandering alone.

Staying connected means staying healthy. For Black men, this means giving ourselves permission to acknowledge and challenge the assumptions that plague us about independence and achievement. The pressures we face are the internalized priorities of financial achievement and success. In this pursuit it can be easy to lose sight of the forest for the trees. Instead of seeking and inviting in opportunities with other Black men, we can often see each other as a threat, a competition of sorts—someone that we must battle if only quietly in our own minds. This can be especially true in professional environments where there is a bloodlust for competitiveness, such as corporate America. This creates little room for honest, authentic connection. You may not realize that in viewing other Black men as threats to your success, you are also cutting off part of yourself that is mirrored in the other. This represents a fundamental miscalculation that as Black men we are not made better by our interconnectedness.

To build connections with other Black men means understanding that you and your brothers are connected. In your journeys throughout life there are synchronicities in which you can see and be seen by one another, offering up a place for momentary refuge. These moments are precious, and you likely don't revel in them enough—perhaps for fear that if you let your guard down and authentically connect, you will somehow be found unworthy and suffer rejection and isolation. In this feared potentiality, you will have to contend with the belief that a brother is somehow more man than you, in whatever ways your mind has convinced you based on your challenges and insecurities. These thoughts are fearful lies inherited from a system built on your disconnection and isolation from others.

You are responsible for challenging any internalized ideas you have about connecting with another Black man and that connection looking a certain way. For many, this means a connection that is superficial—one where you only talk about news items or sports, or the music that's currently most popular. Of course, these topics have value, but so often Black men use these topics to approximate connection rather than experience it, only exacerbating a sense of deep loneliness. If staying connected means staying healthy, then staying superficially connected might mean that you also stay disconnected from yourself, fearful of your own vulnerabilities and weaknesses, imprisoned by the anxiety of being seen.

This is the moment in which you can begin to envision more freedom, and more presence with other men like you. Yes, there is risk for rejection, but unless you try, you're missing out on presence with someone else who is struggling and learning in the same ways you are. Give yourself permission now to open your connections with other Black men more and watch how it feels to be fully present mirrors for one another.

Get Comfortable with Being Uncomfortable

Developing a healthier relationship with the mind and yourself means learning how to hold space for uncomfortable thoughts, feelings, and sensations. Once you arm yourself with the tools to do so, you release yourself from the pressures to always be strong. For a Black man, this means mental freedom.

MEDITATION: I GIVE MYSELF THE SPACE TO SIT WITH DISCOMFORT WITHOUT EXPECTATION.

Has there ever been a time in your life when something tragic happened, like a sudden death or tragic loss, that rocked you? As we get older, the likelihood of facing this kind of grief increases. Take a moment to reflect on your next moves when you learned of your loss. Did you get to the business of executing the tasks that then made sense? Or did you slow down and give yourself the time to cry and grieve? Many of us have moments when we've done either. If we're truly honest with ourselves, we know that in many hard moments we force ourselves to move on much sooner than we actually need to. Yes, we have to take care of the business of life, but that doesn't mean we have to stuff our feelings and tears into little boxes we never examine again. This kind of avoidance, especially as a long-term pattern, isn't healthy for us.

When you take this path of dealing with hardship, you unintentionally minimize your thoughts and feelings. Over time, this becomes the tool you use to avoid any feelings of discomfort. While this may work in the moment, all those little boxes tucked in the back of your conscious mind continue to impact you in covert ways. Frustration and irritability leak out when you least expect it. You may find yourself, in moments, completely disoriented and confused when you spontaneously feel depressed or burst into tears or anger. Those hidden pains burst spontaneously to the surface with no apparent warning, and this might happen at the most inconvenient of times.

The healthier approach is to create space for moments of pain and discomfort to simply exist as they are. This is what it means to "sit with" your feelings. It is often an uncomfortable and painful practice. No one wants to feel pain, yet in this life there is no avoiding it. How do you then go about learning to sit with your discomfort?

Meet your discomfort with mindful nonjudgment. When you dedicate yourself to this meditative practice of being with yourself, within your body and with the breath, you find a sense of peace and catharsis. When you give yourself the moment to simply exist alongside your thoughts and feelings, breathing and inviting in self-compassion and patience, you practice the art of getting comfortable with being uncomfortable. You learn to sit with whatever enters the heart and mind without the pressure to heal or resolve it. In a world that requires Black men to always resist and push forward, these moments of acceptance can be revolutionary. That kind of freedom is a liberation you deserve.

When you give yourself the moment to simply exist alongside your thoughts and feelings, breathing and inviting in self-compassion and patience, you practice the art of getting comfortable with being uncomfortable.

Own Your Story

It can be easy to see ourselves as victims of circumstance. We know that the environment around us impacts us. We are the inheritors of stories from our ancestors and are continually faced with messages in the news and online that try to tell us who we are and what we need. It's time that we start to take our power back.

MEDITATION: I AM THE WRITER OF MY OWN STORY.

We never have ultimate control over our lives, but this does not mean that we have no control. One often overlooked principle in the realm of mental health is the idea of self-determination. Self-determination is our ability to make choices for our own lives. And when we are able to make those choices and find our "why," we move toward our goals. When we are able to self-determine, we feel more aligned, balanced, and grounded. This kind of personal clarity provides direction for our lives and our goals. When we are free to determine for ourselves the life that makes the most sense for us, we find inner peace and fulfillment. Conversely, when we do not find self-determination, we are prone to helplessness. Then we lack purpose, motivation, and clarity on our path.

You've likely come to understand how easily the world can infiltrate your mind and foster helplessness. When you're constantly faced with roadblocks toward your goals and told that you're lazy or not smart enough, or that you'll never be good enough, these psychological harms can be hard to shake. Unfortunately, they often lead to internalization of those ideas and a profound sense of helplessness that squashes your inner desire for self-determination. With all this external noise, and the obligations you find yourself juggling daily, it is an evergreen challenge to be mindful in your connection with yourself, let alone start to craft your own story and direction.

Fortunately, you are more than the stereotypes forced upon you. You are more than the accumulation of your familial inheritance. These parts of you are simply part of your own story. When you start to see yourself as a creator of your life story, and not just the person burdened by others' interpretations and expectations, you learn that you have the power to write your own story.

Where you come from and where you've been are parts of your history, but they do not determine your future. You do. This meditation is the moment of opportunity to pick up the pen and start writing your own story. If you are in control of the direction you take moving forward, what story feels right for you? Of course, no one gets to make these choices in complete isolation, but giving yourself time to reflect on these questions can help you approach your next chapter with more clarity and intention. And where there is clarity, there is the power to manifest and become the man you want to become.

PART 2

Body

It's impossible to talk about mindfulness without exploring the mind-body connection. As mentioned in the introduction of this book, mindfulness is the practice of directing conscious attention to the present moment. This is often difficult for a lot of people due to our reliance on our minds throughout our daily lives. We typically experience the world through our thoughts, rather than our feelings. Of course, there are exceptions to this, but it's frequently the case that we lead with our thoughts and the mind, often at the expense of neglecting our bodies. Overidentification with the mind can lead to intellectualizing our problems and not using our bodies to their fullest benefit.

Your body is an important part of your experience. Not only is it the vessel that allows you to walk through life and experience all the things you do, but it is also an incredible source of data about your internal experience—if you allow yourself to be in connection with it and learn to pay attention to what it can tell you. Practicing mindfulness of the body helps you do just that. After all, the body only exists in the present moment. Therefore, when you pay attention to it, you pay attention to the present moment.

The relationship between Black men and the body is unique. The history around Black bodies is also complex. For Black men, much of that modern history has been centered on viewing the Black man's body as this sort of disidentified entity, like it is not connected to a full human being with depth of thought and feeling. Black men are subject to hypersexual and hypermasculine stereotypes both within and outside of community. These kinds of tropes can feel like compliments when that is all you receive praise for. When your body is only celebrated for its ability to withstand trauma, to carry heavy burdens, and for potential sexual gratification, it's easy to internalize these messages and believe those are the only things the Black male body is good for.

To this, I issue a challenge. In this part, you'll be invited to connect to your body, and yourself, as a source of healing and love. Your arms are made for holding your loved ones to help them feel safe. Your body helps you provide for those you care about. Your body is also there for you to embrace your community in warmth and connection. The meditations in this part are an encouragement to meet your body with gratitude, compassion, and healing.

Start with a Body Scan

Our bodies are the vessels that carry us throughout this world. In this, we recognize that while the body is subjected to the stressors of the world, it also holds the ability for great resilience and healing. Each breath helps the body move forward with more ease. Each step, or moment of action, strengthens our muscles for the next.

MEDITATION: MY BODY IS THE VESSEL THAT CARRIES ME THROUGHOUT THIS WORLD.

Unfortunately for Black folks, our bodies have a long history of mistreatment. Our ancestors survived a level of brutality most of us will never face. Black men's bodies are still highly politicized and are feared and surveilled in ways that other people's aren't. This meditation is an invitation to use your body as a tool for healing. When you do so, it is an act of reclamation. As you move through the meditations in this part, pay attention to how your body responds, and what it may be telling you about your needs and subconscious thoughts or feelings.

This is a practice you can do right now. Place yourself in a comfortable position, whether that means sitting or lying down, and make sure that the environment around you is quiet and calm. When you're practicing body scanning, having less noise and stimulation will help you better tap into your bodily awareness and how it communicates to you.

Take a few breaths and gently inhale through your nose and exhale through your mouth. As you do so, imagine that you're inviting in all the healing air and energy around you. Give yourself permission to be with your breath for a minute as you settle into this moment. Then start to mentally scan your body, starting from the soles of your feet. Take notice of how your feet feel on the floor beneath them. Notice if your feet are relaxed or tense, warm or cold. Focus in on them and try to observe what your body feels like without judging it.

Then shift your focus from your feet up into your calves. Observe whether there is any tightness or tension that you can release on your next breath. Then bring your attention slightly higher up on your leg, toward your knees and thighs. These muscle groups and large tendons in the body tend to work very hard throughout the day, especially if you spend a lot of time standing or moving. As you focus in on this area, envision the healing energy of oxygen moving through it, inviting a release of the tensions felt here.

Now shift your attention further up to your abdomen. The depth of your breath should also come from here. As you take your next breath, allow your belly to expand. In this moment you might become acutely aware of your clothing. You may notice that your pants may feel loose or tight. Your shirt may be resting on your skin as well. Without judging, try to simply notice and observe. Let your breathing anchor you in this space for a moment.

Moving up your body, direct your attention and focus on your chest. When breathing fully, you'll notice the chest expands, opening as if it's inviting peace in as the tension and uneasiness escape with each exhale. As you focus on this area, continue to notice how your breath moves through your body. Next, move your focus up to your arms and shoulders. Observe any discomfort that these parts of your body may be holding right now. Take a moment to acknowledge how your shoulders, arms, hands, and fingers feel.

Continue scanning up the body, switching your focus slightly higher, toward your neck and head. The body often stores stress here. Then bring your focus up to your face and head. As you continue to breathe deeply, notice how your jaw and face feel. Notice if your brow is furrowed or tight. If you notice any tension there, gently let it melt away with the next breath.

Now imagine what it would be like if you could see yourself from a third person point of view. Imagine each breath providing all the oxygen your body needs to heal and move through your daily life with more ease. Allow your body to soften, shoulders falling, as you surrender to this moment.

Offer yourself gratitude for the ability to take this moment to connect with your vessel. Whenever you need to feel grounded in your body, revisit this body scan exercise to reconnect and practice being with yourself in the present moment.

Release Body Shame

Many of us across the diaspora have come to understand our bodies as the vessels that carry us throughout life, yet we are not always kind to them, both in how we nourish and enliven them and in the harmful perspectives we have allowed to take hold in our minds. This is especially true for Black men. By unlearning tired tropes about the Black male form, we can create a healthier connection with these homes on Earth we call bodies.

MEDITATION: MY BODY IS MY HOME, AND IT NEEDS MY RESPECT AND CARE.

How often have you stopped to think of your body as something precious? Not precious as something delicate like a bomb, but something that deserves to be nursed and cared for, like a fledgling plant that needs water, sunlight, and oxygen to grow? It's not common for human beings to stop and think of their bodies in this way, let alone Black men who have been told so many stories about what it means to inhabit a Black body. Many of the stories you unconsciously carry within you, and in this body, are reminiscent of a rich cultural history, for better and for worse.

These legacy notions of Black manhood and masculinity continue to pick away at us in daily ways. Black men, and their bodies, are consistently revered for their strength and size. This has long been the story of Black men in the West. With these stereotypes comes an incredible amount of pressure to live up to a set of ideals, both physically and sexually. These ideals become the standards we internalize and try to fit into at whatever cost. We fail to consider how these messages can be extreme. Not all Black men can possibly fit into this narrow scope of

Black masculinity. For a variety of reasons, these expectations cannot be met by everyone. They run counter to the reality of the variance within a community, and yet we still internalize these ideas. We carry these pressures with us as we age. As we do, these vessels of ours shrink or expand, changing in form or function, often leading us down a path of loathing and feelings of inadequacy.

We encounter these pressures every day in our time spent online, seeing comment sections that either celebrate or shame Black men for fitting in these conscripted molds, or failing to do so, respectively. We live in an age where being a fitness influencer or alpha male biohacker has incredible social clout. The pressures are all around us, and, without even knowing it, we don't realize how these posts and images reinforce these ideas about ourselves and our personal value. We forget these are the same tropes once placed on us and prescribed by folks who bought, abused, and sold us for the same attributes.

Releasing bodily shame starts with the recognition that within you, you carry these tropes. Whether you feel too big, too small, or too long, or come up short, your body is a beautiful, fragile thing. Your body, just like your partner's or your child's, is your home, and you deserve to have a relationship with it that is not hampered by unrealistic expectations that point you in the direction of self-loathing and unworthiness.

This meditation is your opportunity to start to release these expectations placed on you. While they are not of your own creation, these thoughts and beliefs are your responsibility to change. In doing so, you can create a true connection with your body rooted in deep care and respect rather than shame and guilt for not being, or looking, how everyone else demands you to look. Your body is not a machine, and neither are you. You are more than that. You deserve to be nurtured and cared for.

Invest in this relationship with your body by challenging each thought that reduces you into parts for admiration or consumption.

Give yourself the permission now to be whole just as you are, without qualification.

Your body is not a machine, and neither are you. You are more than that. You deserve to be nurtured and cared for.

Meet Your Body with Gratitude

In the previous meditation, you explored the relationship that Black men have with unrealistic body expectations. Filtered down through historical lessons, these stereotypes can be at times inspiring, but at other times shaming and rooted in self-deprecation. But what does it mean to go further and create a relationship with the body that centers gratitude? It means taking the time to acknowledge and thank your body for the way it carries you throughout the world.

MEDITATION: I AM THANKFUL FOR THE POWER AND PRESENCE OF EMBODIMENT.

One of the challenges of getting older is the recognition that our bodies are not able to do what they used to. This realization can be devastating for a lot of folks, especially Black men. As our bodies change in their capacity for strength and endurance, as is natural with aging, we come face-to-face with our mortality and humanity. We are faced with the recognition that Black male bodies also change over time, and in ways that we're often uncomfortable with.

Our bodies' functions change, and that is a normal part of development throughout life. But aging isn't the only time in which we experience challenges with our bodies. When we are faced with illness and injury, we also come face-to-face with the changing capacity of our bodies, especially if this change is serious or chronic. Whether due to natural aging or sickness and disease, maintaining a healthy mindset and relationship with your body is a challenge when it no longer fits the internal script of strength you've carried for most of your life. Instead of only living in the grief of your changing body, mindfulness allows you to meet your body with gratitude for how it is right now.

Often in the practice of mindfulness, there is a sense of calm and peacefulness that you may not otherwise experience in your life. It's a shame really, given that most waking hours are not spent living in this space of mindful intention. When you get to the place of presence, it often illuminates the pains and challenges you're currently carrying both mentally and physically, which is why so many avoid it. And yet, there is a magic to mindfulness that in some of those moments in practice, when you are connected to the moment and the breath, the rest of the world falls away and all you are left with is the truth of your being, a sense of who you are as whole, full human being who is part of a world broader than daily stressors and challenges. That connection can be beautiful.

It is this idea that you may forget is also available to you at any point in time. While it can be difficult to accept the ways in which you experience challenge navigating your daily life, and the changing nature of the vessel that carries you through it, you can still acknowledge what is good in these moments of mindful connection with your body. It's not an effort in gaslighting, but an invitation to get connected to the fullness of life that exists in each moment. If you acknowledge the ways in which your body changes and is challenging for you, you can also make a conscious effort to draw attention to the good and the abilities you still have in each moment. The two do not cancel each other out but can peacefully coexist as reminders of Black men's complexity as human beings.

Even with illness, disease, or energy, there is still the opportunity to be thankful for what your body is still able to do. You can honor both the challenges and the gifts that your body affords you in each moment. Meeting the body with gratitude can look like saying "thank you" to your body after a workout. It can also look like having an intention to honor it with a nourishing or enjoyable meal. Practicing gratitude with your body can look like bathing and grooming yourself regularly. It can also look like extending it grace, allowing it to rest for a moment when it nudges you for relief and ease. Use this meditation to meet yourself, and your body, with gratitude daily and watch how your relationship with it shifts over time.

View Vulnerability As Strength

When did the word "vulnerability" become a four-letter word? For men, vulnerability is often thought of as a weakness or symbol of frailty, but vulnerability can offer us so much more, if we allow it. In this meditation you are invited to reflect on how vulnerability provides for the flexibility needed to help us strengthen our bodies, better adapt to the world around us, and even thrive in our lives.

MEDITATION: I ALLOW MYSELF TO BEND BUT NOT BREAK.

When you think of the word "vulnerable," what are the thoughts and images that come to mind? For many Black men, we associate being vulnerable with being weak or frail. It's not hard to take this kind of black-and-white stance, as it is the story so many of us are brought up in. It's no wonder why so many of us find ourselves drawn into the pages of and ideas in stoicism; we have already been primed for its tenets through our experiences growing up. We are raised and taught that to feel pain is to be weak, so we spend a lot of time convincing ourselves that we are not in pain, as our bodies (and minds) fall apart, and we subject those around us to live with the rubble.

But vulnerability is more than weakness; it is resilience and adaptability. No one is always formidable and strong. Unfortunately, Black men have inherited, and internalized, the idea that to acknowledge harm or trauma is akin to being a victim. And we often blame and shame victims for their own plights even if we don't say so aloud. We still have a long way to go until we see vulnerability for what it truly is . . . a strength.

It takes courage and strength to acknowledge your vulnerability, especially in a world that tries its damnedest daily to convince you that if you're not the apex predator, then you are the prey. And whoever wants to think of themselves as potential prey? This ill-informed perspective keeps the body and nervous system in a constant state of vigilance, always looking to protect itself from whatever competition or threat lies just around the corner. It is draining and harmful to the body, as well as the mind and spirit.

Think of the humble rubber band. It is not rigid. It has the ability to stretch and shrink depending on what's needed of it at the time. It is flexible enough to know how to adapt to novel situations and tasks when it's called upon for help. And yet, it also has its limits. When stretched too far and too much, it snaps into self-destruction. You can take a cue from the humble rubber band as you think of your own vulnerability. It's normal and valid to honor your ability to shrink and stretch depending on the situation at hand; you are not always meant to work at maximum potential. For the sustainability of the rubber band, and your own, you must admit there is a limit. You must, at times, contract and rest. You must give yourself permission to acknowledge the risk of self-destruction. Practice the strength needed to honor your vulnerability before you snap in two and are never the same again.

Connect to the Healing Breath

Our bodies are the vessels that carry us throughout the world we live in. Once we recognize the power of our bodies to create a sense of grounding and healing, we learn that we are never without the capacity for inner peace and stillness. A practice of connecting with the breath means connecting to the parts of ourselves always capable of moving forward and healing despite whatever pain or challenge we've been through.

MEDITATION: WITH EACH BREATH I AM HEALING AND BECOMING MORE RESILIENT.

The breath is an underused tool for managing health and wellness. We take for granted that breathing is something we do automatically. We forget it is a complex physiological process that can help us bridge the body and mind in profound ways. Mindful breathing allows us to explore and connect with ourselves in new ways. There is a lot of power in Black men leaning into strategies that can help us navigate the challenging world around us, with all of its expectations and pressures. When we create moments to connect with the breath, we transition from waking states of consciousness to deep connection with a sense of living and being without interruption or distraction.

Mindful breathing is always accessible to you. When you are ready to create a moment of healing for yourself, you need to place yourself in an environment that is quiet and where you can feel secure. Get yourself comfortable and then allow yourself to notice your body in the space. Are there certain points of strain or tension as you sit? Also, take note of what you observe may be going through your mind as you start to settle in. It's common for plenty of thoughts to come up as you start a practice of noticing during mindful breathing. The mind is often so busy, but for many, this busy nature only becomes apparent when actually slowing down and embracing mindfulness. In this meditation, practice envisioning any of these busy, pressured thoughts as small leaves that blow away in a gentle breeze until they are out of sight.

Black men don't always have the privilege of honoring ourselves. It can be difficult to create the time and space we deserve to practice self-healing. With a mindful breathing practice, you are giving yourself an important gift. This healing breath practice can offer you moments of sanctuary. You can always connect with your breath mindfully when you need more balance and grounding.

This is the moment you will begin to intentionally shift your breathing from automatic to a more intentional process. Inhale through your nose, taking in all the air from the room around you. As you do, you can imagine a sense of lightness entering into your lungs as it expands your chest and stomach. As you exhale, try letting the air out gently over the course of a few seconds, instead of letting it all out at once.

Continue this alternating process of mindfully inhaling and exhaling over the next few minutes. With each cycle of inhale and exhale, try to extend the breath until you find a pace and length that feels like intentional effort but not so strenuous as to leave you feeling exhausted. Connecting to the healing breath is effortful and takes focus, but it should be restorative, not exhausting. As you spend a few minutes in this simple practice of inhaling and exhaling, you're connecting with your natural capacity to heal and recover from whatever challenges you're carrying.

This practice of mindful breathing can take as long or as little as you like. Most people benefit from at least five minutes of practice daily. This gives your mind a bit of time to settle in and focus on the breath instead of whatever else may be occupying you. Whether this takes you five or fifteen minutes, make sure you have the time and space you need for healing.

With each breath, you become more mindful and more resilient. Mindful breathing, while simple, is an act of connecting the brain and heart, creating space for you to practice self-care whenever, and wherever, you may need it.

Mindful breathing, while simple, is an act of connecting the brain and heart, creating space for you to practice self-care whenever, and wherever, you may need it.

Define Success on Your Own Terms

Even though often unspoken, there are many rules that Black men are supposed to live by. In order to be seen as someone of value and worth, success becomes defined not by who we are, but by what we have. Releasing some of this pressure, and defining success for yourself, can have a profound positive impact on your inner peace.

MEDITATION: I DEFINE SUCCESS ON MY OWN TERMS.

It's of no surprise that when asked about how they define success, most people mention money. Money is the fuel for most things in our world, and certainly within the West. Preoccupation with money requires us to prioritize human productivity and economic gain over wellness. For its luster we sacrifice our mental health, and sometimes even life and limb, to achieve a distorted promise of the American dream.

For Black men, dreams of ultimate financial success are born from a nightmare. The cultural machine that had our ancestors on auction blocks is, unfortunately, still the same metric by which we can often prioritize our definition of success. The message in which we've invested is that our value as men is only as deep as our pockets, only as lengthy as our bank account numbers, and we may be willing to sacrifice all else for this ultimate validation. This leads to overwork and taxing the body beyond its ability to repair and heal.

Part of the motivation for focusing on accumulating wealth is righteous. Coming from cultural and collective poverty in the West, scarcity can motivate us to achieve and acquire more than we ever thought possible. The aim can be to secure family security for generations. This is a noble venture, but it can still produce the kind of pressure that is quiet in its internal destruction of our bodies (and minds). You work endlessly to reach a financial goal that never is enough. It's not sustainable and too taxing on the body.

When your view of success is attached solely to monetary value, it is a recipe for failure, and even physical illness. Just as money comes, so can it go. These sudden shifts often happen when you least expect them. When you are defined by this type of success and worth and lose it, who are you then? Who do you become when circumstances cause your definition of success to fall like a house of cards? The impact is devastating.

You need money to be successful in this life, but what if there was more to your success than simply what you could earn? Could you begin to consider a fuller perspective on what it means to be fulfilled and successful, where money or accolades are but one part of a bigger equation? Take the next few moments to meditate on how you may begin to balance your goals for wealth and offering your body the care it needs and deserves.

Success can be anything you make it. It can be about promotions and monetary value, but it can also be about a sense of compassion for yourself. Success could be measured in your commitments to a partner or children. Success can be contributing to your community and the world around you. Success can be all things, and it is up to you to decide. Who will you be when the winds of a materialistic world threaten the dollars and cents? You will be more than what you have, because you already are.

Discover Your Life's Purpose and Ambition

When we enter this world, we inherit so much. Not only do we inherit the dreams and wishes of our parents and family, but we also find ourselves unknowingly thrust into society's expectations. From who we are to who we will be in the future, we have many choices to make in becoming. Mindfulness meditation can help you gain clarity and make these choices as you use your body to turn away from external noise and tune into the feedback your body provides.

MEDITATION: I GIVE MYSELF THE GIFT OF EXPLORATION TO DISCOVER MY LIFE'S PATH.

One of the greatest challenges to achieving a sense of internal peace and stillness is learning to navigate the world around us mindfully. We must learn to manage external stimuli consciously. At times, outside noise can be so disruptive that it becomes difficult to tune into ourselves. We may even forget that we have a voice, and a choice, in where we direct our focus and attention. This means that we have to sift through an incredible amount of noise to even begin listening to ourselves. Mindfulness provides a window for us to use the body as a tool to reflect with less outside noise and influence, and visualize our deepest ambitions.

For Black men, learning to listen to that internal voice can be a challenge due to pressure we face from those around us. When mothers, sisters, partners, and family members have a stake in what they see as right for us, pressure can mount. When that feedback is so routine, and the messages themselves are consistent over time, those voices turn into our own. The messages passed on to us easily become the ways we measure our own success. They become the rules by which we define our purpose and ambitions in this world.

These messages also come from the environment around us. Consider the amount of Internet videos and podcasts we encounter in any given week. This content, along with the ads that accompany it, is designed to steal our attention. Influencers are meant to influence. Once they have our focus, then they're able to reinforce their perspectives on what a man's purpose and ambitions are supposed to be. Often they use fear to go about their convincing. You will know that is happening if you can learn to pay attention to your body as you are watching and listening to these things. Do you start to feel uneasy or restless? Do your emotions start to point toward urgency and competitiveness? If so, they've done their job in convincing you that their message is the truth and the way to a life worth living. Unchallenged, these messages easily become the criteria for Black men seeing themselves as worthy and man enough.

In contrast, this meditation offers you an invitation. It's far less exciting and far less programmed, but in it is more truth. Give yourself a moment to sit and reflect on all those messages you've been receiving about what it means to be successful and what it means to be a man. Take notice of how this feels in your body and what thoughts run through your mind as you reflect. Do the thoughts and feelings that come up feel encouraging and supportive and lighten how you feel in your body? Or do self-critical thoughts and shame show up as sensations of heaviness and restlessness to motivate you?

Shame is not a healthy motivator. There is another way, a kinder way, to motivate yourself. In this moment of reflection, imagine that these messages and stories start to fade away in the background. Visualize the messages going from being in front of you, like seeing them through a car windshield, to something you can only see through side mirrors or your rearview as you continue to drive forward. They simply fade into the background. As the distance grows, imagine arriving at the bank of a river. You're there, alone and in self-reflection. You have a sifter tool that allows you to search for gold and other precious minerals. Picture yourself picking up that tool, submerging it into the river's water, and shaking it. As you raise it out of the river, you're left with small gold nuggets bearing your personal ambitions. What do those precious little stones say? When you are alone and panning for them, what is revealed to you? This is what it means to discover your own life's purpose and ambition.

Now you get to decide what to do with them.

Build Resilience in the Face of Adversity

At its best, resilience offers us the hope that there is possible relief beyond the current hurt we experience. On the other hand, overutilizing resilience can often result in minimization of our pain, forcing us to move through, and on from, our experiences without so much of a beat between injury and resolution. But with mindful intention we can find the balance that allows for presence in adversity.

MEDITATION: I AM DISCOVERING RESILIENCE THROUGH ACTIONS ON MY OWN TERMS.

Unfortunately, much of what we have been taught about the Black experience has been rooted in the stories of our collective struggle. Our history, if we are ever fortunate enough to learn morsels of it, briefly focuses on the atrocities of enslavement in the Western part of the world, and the often-sanitized stories of civil rights heroes that helped us gain the rights we find ourselves fervently fighting for again right now. This offers the question: "How can mindfulness provide a pathway for us to build resilience in the face of adversities that continue to challenge our progress at every step?"

Building resilience relies on two foundational truths: meaningful rest and right action. While the work of challenging the harmful status quos of racism, ableism, homophobia, etc., is necessary, we mustn't forget that as we desire to wage war on these "isms," we are concurrently injured by their swords. Racism triggers long-held stories of Black inferiority, ableism mirrors concerns about our own capacity to live and thrive, and homophobia triggers questions about the nuances of our thoughts and feelings on gender and sexuality. With these "isms" comes doubt and pain even if we intellectually come to understand the attacks hurled aren't ultimately true. And what helps manage an injury? Rest and healing. Moments spent in mindful reflection and peaceful connection with the self can create refuge in an easeful space we don't otherwise experience in this great, challenging world of ours. We must take a moment to tend to our wounds, and the impact these injuries have on our bodies. These stressors harm the nervous system and can manifest in the body as muscle tension, fatigue, stomach upset, chest pains, and more. The body needs rest and recovery to heal.

In addition to rest, it is necessary for you to find the right actions for you to fight adversity. One thing people often get wrong about "the work" is the belief that it looks the same for everyone. It's important to remember that with any action you take, you must take into consideration the impact on your body and the fullness of your life and responsibilities. Right action should be configured in such a way that it enables you, especially as a Black man, to be physically and emotionally present for those who also depend on you in their daily lives. There can be no "right action" without consideration of these facts.

Figuring out what is accessible and sustainable action to challenge adversity is an individual pursuit. You may have already begun to consider what actions feel right for you. If not, this meditation is another opportunity to take a few mindful breaths, close your eyes, and ask yourself the question, "What do I need to find resilience in this moment?" Then give yourself permission to fully listen.

Moments spent in mindful reflection and peaceful connection with the self can create refuge in an easeful space we don't otherwise experience in this great, challenging world of ours.

Heal a Parental Wound

When we come into the world, we are born into families and environments not of our choosing. While it is difficult to acknowledge the fullness of our inheritance, mindfully allowing ourselves to honor the truths of our experience can help us experience a deep sense of compassion and care for ourselves. It can also give us space to extend compassion to our parents who weren't able to get everything right.

MEDITATION: BY ACKNOWLEDGING MY WOUNDS, I CREATE SPACE FOR THEIR HEALING.

Even the best of parents gets things wrong. Sometimes they don't have the resources, or support, themselves to give their children all that children deserve. It is our task, as adults who are growing and healing, to mind the gap between what we wanted or felt we deserved, and what we received. This intergenerational conflict is as natural as birth itself. We need not be shamed for any pain, anger, or resentment we may carry from childhood. This pain does not define our lives either. We can make space for both.

In this meditation, you will make space for both pain and healing. As with any practice, it is important to create a time and space in which you can fully focus on your practice and nothing else. With mindfulness you can always do this with the breath, mindfully inhaling and exhaling, and taking a few minutes to get grounded in your body. The breath is your gateway to the present moment.

When you feel grounded within yourself, start to reflect on the relationship with your father or any paternal figure(s) who helped raise you. Think of his energy, his posture, and his way of being. Start to contemplate the messages you received from him about what it means to be a Black man in this world. Consider what behavior he modeled for you, in his relationships with you and others around him. Consider the ways in which he showed up with your mother or any other partners. Reflect on his sense of emotional vulnerability or openness. These were your first lessons of what it meant to be a man in this world. What did you learn or inherit? What are you now noticing in your body as you consider this?

Now you can reflect on your relationship with your mother or any maternal figure(s) who helped raise you. Think of how she moved throughout the world. Reflect on early memories you had with her and how she treated you. Consider whether she treated you with care and attention or presented as cold or distant at times when you needed her. What lessons did you learn from her about relationships and women? As you reflect on this relationship, what sensations show up in your body?

As you sit in contemplation of those lessons, give yourself the permission to acknowledge any discrepancies between them and what you now know would have been more helpful for you. It's often the case that the deepest vulnerabilities or concerns in relationships have roots in early life experiences. These vulnerabilities show up in the body when triggered. Feelings of mistrust, anxiety around connecting, or even fears around abandonment may manifest with stomach discomfort all the way up to rising tension and tightness in the chest and around the heart. If you are noticing any sensations now, give yourself the space to feel them and continue mindful breathing to help ground and soothe you.

It can be difficult to reflect on your past in this way. After all, there is a reason why you may sometimes avoid this kind of presence with yourself; at times mindfulness can make you face uncomfortable feelings you would much rather avoid. If this is true for you, know that what you are thinking and feeling is valid. Anger and resentment may come up as you sit in this kind of reflection. You may also feel compassion and sympathy for the challenges you know got in the way of your parents being the kinds of caregivers you needed at times. Mindfulness gives you the freedom to not judge the variety of feelings you feel. Anger and sympathy, however disorienting, can coexist in the space of mindfulness. Mindfulness makes space for the entirety of your truth.

Every Black boy deserves safety, protection, and care. Within you is an inner child (which you will meditate on in Part 3) who still wants the validation, care, space, and encouragement from your parents. In these kinds of meditations, you're creating space for more compassion toward yourself and any unresolved feelings that may continue to linger. It is important to see the revelations and insights you have here as invitations for further internal conversation. These are lessons you can take with you, for your own good, but also for the health of your relationships and any family you may make of your own.

Your parental wounds do not define you. Let them inspire you to live with more self-compassion.

Embrace Change As a Path to Growth

Life can be challenging. As it presents its unanticipated twists and turns, we can find ourselves in cycles of pain and discontent. We intellectually understand that we are not able to control our world entirely, and yet the discomfort of living through these changes and challenges can be incredibly hard on us. At times, we may find ourselves confused on our next steps.

MEDITATION: I GIVE MYSELF PERMISSION TO EMBRACE CHANGE AS A PATH TO GROWTH.

Human beings don't like change, especially when we are not in direct control of it. When the tides of our lives turn, and we are forced to deal with them, we easily become disoriented and confused about our life's direction. Then comes frustration, anxiety, and irritability because we believe that things were fine before the change. This very well may be true. We also convince ourselves we are okay with things when we're actually not. We retreat from the effort and discomfort that improvement requires from us. We can resign ourselves to the familiarity of the good instead of going for the great because of the risks involved.

This apprehension, if not outright rejection of change, is normal and yet it can also be dysfunctional. It can force you to contort your body (and mind) in accepting a reality that is familiar even if not comfortable. You may interpret the physical symptoms of fear (increased heart rate, higher blood pressure, tension in the body, etc.) as signals to avoid the risk that comes with change. What is familiar becomes what is safe, and anything that begins to threaten that sense of safety, like change, you may meet with aggression and defensiveness.

The body carries that stress and tension. You continue to avoid the fear, and miss the opportunity for growth. For Black men in particular, the discomfort in navigating change, and being forced to embrace being an unskilled beginner, can trigger deep feelings of inadequacy. Change is hard because it brings you face-to-face with the shame you have with not knowing, a pressure with which most men must contend. This shame brings a heaviness to the body that further fuels demotivation and avoidance, keeping you stuck. You don't have to approach change in this way. Change can lead you into a new, and necessary, era of your life.

One of the simplest examples of this you can find in the natural world is the changing of the seasons. Each season (spring, summer, fall, and winter) brings about its own unique characteristics. They each have their own time to shine. As a hemisphere of Earth reaches its spring equinox, the perils of winter fade further away, making way for equal amounts of daylight and nighttime. The change allows for more beauty, allowing flowers to reemerge for the next period of their life cycle. Each season has its own positives and negatives, and yet still finds its place in the natural order, allowing change to inspire growth and novelty.

In this you learn from the natural world that change, even metaphorical death, doesn't just have to mean suffering and termination. Change can mean new beginnings. Change can bring opportunities for inspiration and growth. While the moments of transition can be hard to navigate, they can also be your natural shepherds into the next place in which you are meant to be. That is, only if you allow yourself to be moved. Meditate on your capacity to manage fear through this practice of mindfulness. Give yourself permission to weather the emotional storm on the way into your next season.

Trust Your Strength to Overcome Challenges

In English translations of the principles of Buddhism, one phrase often sticks out. That phrase is that "life is suffering." While this adage is incomplete in its translation, according to religious and spiritual scholars, most of us have lived long enough to understand that with life come periods of challenge. However, this truth that with life comes suffering is coupled with a deeper truth: We are all also capable of meeting life's challenges.

MEDITATION: I AM LEARNING TO TRUST MY STRENGTH TO CARRY ME THROUGH.

When faced with the challenges of life, we are reminded that with joy there is also, at times, hurt and pain. We do our best to navigate the more routine responsibilities and obligations of life when met with more sporadic and intense challenges, such as illness and death. These challenges can be painful in and of themselves. Our suffering is also complicated by our interpretation of life's hard moments as well. When hurt lands on our doorstep, we strain ourselves by wishing the injury wasn't real in the first place. We often forgo giving our bodies the rest necessary to recover and instead push our bodies through pain. This limits our capacity to meet future challenges with the necessary strength and resilience.

Most of us have faced many challenges, sometimes in quick succession. These can leave on us long-standing imprints of trauma and pain. We may suffer through poverty and malnourishment. We may suffer from physical illness and injury that demand adjustments to life moving forward. Stress can leave the nervous system in a constant state of fatigue. When these challenges accumulate, it is difficult for the body to bounce back. All of these can contribute to a feeling that life, in all its glory, is suffering and unfair. As we try to make sense of our cumulative pain, a sense of helplessness and nihilism can overwhelm any effort to continue to live or thrive. And it is in these moments that we forget our innate strength and capacity to heal and recover through rest.

This descent into darkness is something that each human experiences at one point or another, however brief. These periods of deep challenges are not only faced by us as individuals, but also as communities and cultures. Such is the case of folks across the African Diaspora. Whether due to the atrocities encountered on the motherland through colonization or trauma endured on Western shores, all Black men carry within us a legacy of those challenges. When faced with an ongoing onslaught of challenges in present life, we can forget that within those histories there is also a legacy of strength and perseverance. We face continued obstacles in visiting with the legacy of resilience, as others might wish we forget that we are much more than our suffering.

In moments of present-centered mindfulness, you can be reminded of this strength. Even in times in which vulnerability ventures into weakness and thoughts of self-defeat, you must remember that there is also strength. The next heartbeat, and each subsequent breath in your body, is a reminder that within you there is a life force, power, and strength left. As oxygen enters each muscle and organ, you are invited to remember all that you are capable of. In every moment that follows inner turmoil, struggle, or pain, you will then meet the following moment as a reminder of your ability to overcome whatever challenge lies in your way.

Don't forget to give yourself the gift of these meditative moments of rest and the ability to remember who you, and your people, have always been. Taking a moment to pause and be with yourself offers a reminder of not only the strength of your lineage, but also all the ways in which you've steeled yourself through every hardship you've faced before in your own experiences. You have more strength than you consciously know. Within you there is a survivor capable of great things. Yes, life is suffering, but your life is also supported by the strength and spirit within each moment.

You have more strength than you consciously know. Within you there is a survivor capable of great things.

Transform Pain Into Power

What is pain if not the acknowledgment of harm perpetuated against our very being? To acknowledge pain means to acknowledge the reality of life, which can be unjust and harmful at times. And yet, we find some ways to recover and move forward. Within us lies the possibility to honor the pain of our injuries, and use the next moments as opportunities for transforming pain into power.

MEDITATION: BY ACKNOWLEDGING MY PAIN, I FORGE A PATH TO HEAL.

Unfortunately, these days it is easy to see the pain all around us. There is constant war, disease and illness, and political authoritarianism in communities around the world. In addition, there has never been a more toxic place than the Internet. With all their glee in abusive language and trolling, the Internet and social media provide spaces for us to project onto one another our wounds in public fashion. For Black men, and People of Color more broadly, the challenges of such a world cannot be overstated. There is an ongoing rise of fascism and racist sentiments that we must endure, despite our best efforts to shield ourselves from these harsh realities daily.

Too often have Black men been subjected to the stereotypes and lies about their desire and aggression. And in these stereotypes society has told us that Black men do not suffer. This message has been so ubiquitous that Black men ourselves wear this badge of "unaffected" with pride, knowing that it is a performance. And the performance is a lie.

The truth that we are harmed by the realities of prejudice, racism, etc., is not a weakness; it is simply reality. And when you can take the moment to acknowledge the impact, of course you will find yourself sitting with the suffering of it, but this moment also offers an opportunity for a conscious choice of how to respond to your pain. Will you choose to be the man who continues to harm because he has been harmed, or will you recognize these feelings as invitations to cultivate resilience and use this reclamation of power as a tool for healing?

There is no singular salve that can provide protection from this painful reality. But mindfulness provides a path to transform pain into power. In this meditation you are invited to first practice acknowledgment and acceptance of the pain you've experienced. Racial stress can often lead to high blood pressure and heart problems. Alternatively, you may also experience the drain of hypervigilance on your nervous system as you socially and physically shrink to survive or achieve. You can moderate this impact first by acknowledging and accepting these challenges. Naming your pain is often the first step in healing. As you acknowledge this impact, you may feel more able to allow yourself to tend to your wounds.

In this moment, you can bring yourself back to the healing power of your breath. You may stretch to relieve the tension in your body or simply cross your arms over your chest, offering yourself a self-soothing hug as you recite the meditation "By acknowledging my pain, I forge a path to heal." This moment is the space to offer your body the care it needs. This healing is helping you to remember that within you, you always hold the ability to transform pain into power.

When you take these moments to honor your pain, you create the opportunity for healing yourself. This healing may allow you to extend your hand outward to seek the comfort and support you need, or it may even allow you to extend your hand outward to the brother next to you to show him a path of healing where pain is a bump in his path. There is power in acknowledging the injuries of life and letting that inform your next steps that are expansive and progressive, instead of nihilistic and resigned to defeat.

Your story of pain is also the story of power if you so choose it.

Ground Your Body in Moments of Uncertainty

When we are surrounded by uncertainty and chaos, it is natural to feel overwhelmed with anxiety and restlessness in anticipation of what's to come. Existing in these moments is difficult, and at times can be paralyzing. It is in these moments that we need the ability and space to ground our bodies in a safe space. This grounding can be profoundly relieving when the future is unclear.

MEDITATION: I SLOW DOWN AND ALLOW THE BREATH TO GROUND ME IN THIS MOMENT.

Uncertainty is one of life's most ordinary realities. And somehow, as human beings, we often find it difficult to navigate moments where there is a lack of clarity. Emotionally, uncertainty is something we struggle with as it can lead to feelings of worry and anxiety. Uncertainty is often accompanied by ruminating thoughts about what is yet to come and what you'll need to do about it when that future moment comes. These experiences, the rumination, worry, and anxiety, aren't often talked about with respect to Black men. This is likely true because anxiety and worry may not look on us how it does on others. If our posture is often relaxed and cool, whether authentic or some sort of expected projection of calm, the result is the same: Anxiety is often hard to read on Black men, and we don't often recognize it for what it is. This makes it even more difficult to address said anxiety. For Black men, this anxiety may not appear as conscious worry, but more so like increased irritability or hostility. The body can manifest this through restless movements and tension, as well as shallow breathing or tightness in the chest, back, or other areas of the body. Mindfulness provides us an opportunity to draw attention to our uneasiness and respond with compassion. In doing so, we develop our capacity for grounding and refuge.

When was the last time you recognized what you were dealing with was anxiety? Odds are it may have been difficult to recognize. It won't always look like a racing heart, or sweating in nervousness, or sound like what others may describe as "worrying." Anxiety in Black men may look like shaking your leg or tapping your fingers when you're otherwise relaxing. Anxiety can also look like being more irritable or short with others even though nothing is obviously wrong. The manifestations of anxiety can look different on everyone. The sad truth is, for a lot of people, they've long gotten used to anxiety within their bodies, and have trouble seeing it in themselves when it needs their attention the most. Fortunately, giving yourself some time to self-reflect can provide you with the clues you need to understand your experience. And once you start to recognize these physical symptoms as the anxiety that they are, you can start to use mindfulness to ground yourself when you need.

At times, this meditative self-reflection in itself can be grounding enough. Simply asking yourself, "Is that what worrying looks like for me?" can be the wake-up call to take further action to care for yourself. At other times, that awareness is but the first step toward a more grounded experience.

And what does grounding look like in practice? Mindfulness teaches that presence is the key to being connected with yourself. That is, you can experience grounding by first slowing down and offering yourself the moment to check in. Following your reflection, close your eyes and take a few slow, deep breaths and practice truly being with yourself. Rather than fighting for an answer to help you avoid the discomfort you may be feeling, slow down and listen. By listening, you're able to recognize that the moment of grounding is here, in the moment of breathing and being. Grounding is in this moment you give yourself permission to honor what it is you're feeling.

Yes, this may seem simple, but slowing down and listening isn't always easy. This is why mindfulness exercises like meditation take practice. The good news is that the more you use this muscle of pausing, you'll start to feel the grounding and sense of centeredness that comes along with it more easily. And with that, you open up your body (and mind) to uncover what solutions or strategies were there all along, only covered up by your worry and restlessness.

Find a safe space, plant yourself as if you were a tree with strong roots, and pay attention to the inner wisdom and peace that unlocks in that moment.

Redefine Black Masculinity

What it means to be a man is a hot topic in our current world. A cacophony of voices, particularly those online, are at the forefront of these conversations, often putting out extreme points of view to garner views and clicks. Black men find ourselves challenged by these conversations. But as we continue to evolve as a people, we can learn to redefine and embody Black masculinity for ourselves.

MEDITATION: I HAVE THE POWER TO CREATE MASCULINITY ON MY OWN TERMS.

If you were to ask anyone about what it looks like to be a Black man, you may hear a lot of things that we generally think of as positive. The stereotype of Black masculinity is often someone who is cool, calm, and collected. A Black man is someone who doesn't buckle under pressure and handles his business without fanfare or celebration. On the other hand, there are also stereotypes of Black men as more aggressive, hostile, and sexualized than men of other races. These messages reference a long history of the white ruling class creating a mythical boogeyman to project onto all their fears, fantasies, and hidden desires. Unfortunately, these ideas have been internalized over time. We feel pressure to be those hypermasculine, hyperindependent, and hypersexualized figures. But we have power in self-defining what manhood can look for us and how we choose to embody it.

In order to redefine Black masculinity, you must first define it. When you're in an environment that feels conducive to more thoughtful introspection, reflect on how you've experienced the pressures of masculinity in your own life. Consider what manhood has meant to you. You may start by reflecting on the expectations society has for Black men. How does this society define masculinity? In what ways are Black men taught to navigate work and professional life and what are the roles that are positioned as success? Consider the pressure and urgency that might come along with those expectations.

As you continue to explore through this meditation, consider the relationships that you have been taught to have with yourself and others as a Black man. Is it normal and expected for you to have a practice of self-reflection (and one that doesn't involve prioritizing money)? How are you taught to respond to your own emotions, and how are you supposed to respond to other men in your life when they are struggling? Give yourself the space to consider if these same expectations provide freedom and relief or stress and a sense of limitation. Ground yourself in this moment of deep reflection and begin to ask yourself the question, "What would it take, and what would need to change about my view of masculinity, in order for me to feel more grounded, whole, and more at ease?" The answer may start with giving yourself the freedom to think beyond what you've known thus far on this journey of life.

Imagine that you could live in a world in which you could honor what feels true about your own definition of masculinity and enables you to feel supported and more at peace in those moments when you need it. Consider a future in which you have the time and energy to focus on what's most important to you, and not on what the world says you must focus. Create a mental picture of the friendships, romantic relationships, and family connections that could manifest by your own new rules. What changes would you make to ensure this vision becomes a reality? Would you use different words or language in how you communicate with others?

Would your style or posture change as you walk through the world? How would you not only redefine masculinity internally, but also embody this redefinition in your daily life? As you meditate on these questions, observe any sensations within your body and what it may be telling you about your journey forward. Any changes that you make can require a lot of energy, focus, and intention. Perhaps not all these changes are possible at once, but this is an invitation to consider how you would move differently if you felt it possible to create this more fulfilling life for yourself.

You have the power to start creating a world around you that feels more aligned with your definition of masculinity. Now is the moment the world also requires change from within you that you can put out into your environment. You have the strength and the capacity to merge these two worlds into a more aligned, and physical, reality.

Use this meditation as the inspiration to embody changes you'd like to make in your life.

You have the power to start creating a world around you that feels more aligned with your definition of masculinity.

Challenge Toxic Masculinity Within and Around You

When the term "toxic masculinity" entered the zeitgeist years ago, it was meant to reference a toxic sense of manhood that prioritizes control and aggression over others, leaving a path of harm in its wake. Unfortunately, the term devolved into a catchall phrase hurled at any men engaged in changing definitions of socially undesirable behavior. As the world continues to deal with its evolving definitions, it is up to us to continue to challenge what toxic, and what healthy, masculinity can mean.

MEDITATION: I WILL STAND STRONG IN CHALLENGING TOXIC MASCULINITY WITHIN AND AROUND ME.

In the natural and scientific worlds, when a substance is labeled as toxic, it means it causes harm. Its influence can be particularly insidious, especially if not appropriately addressed and remedied. We see this process of identification of toxic ingredients by regulatory agencies to protect citizens from ingredients or substances that may have unanticipated effects. Yet when it comes to the idea of toxic masculinity, we continue to struggle with accurately identifying it and challenging its influence. We ignore the pain, the stress on the body, and the risky behaviors associated with it. It is in part because of how we see masculinity within ourselves as Black men.

Rather than looking at masculinity as negative on the whole, take a moment to examine the impact it has on you and on the lives of others. Does your sense of masculinity guide you into the perils of overworking your body—to the point of your sleep and health suffering? Does it put you in regular conflict with partners and other loved ones who request more of your presence and attention? Does this sense of masculinity mean ignoring the needs of those same loved ones, and even yourself even as the tension and stress worsens your health? If so, it's time to challenge your ideas and definitions of what masculinity truly means.

Mindfulness and connection to nature provide you with an opportunity to visit with the natural world and see the natural variance within a species. Nature also provides you with examples of the ebb and flow of strength and vulnerability. These concepts are natural to you as a sophisticated animal, yet at times you may forgo these understandings for the sake of ego-identified success and achievement. But no one is immune from what is natural to their being. Just as the seasons change, so do you. Leaves fall and die as a cooler season arrives. Snakes shed their skin and birds molt their feathers. These are all examples of healthy natural change that you can emulate. There are seasons in life. So can there be seasons of what it means to be a man. You can, and need to, evolve for survival in the natural world. You can also feel emboldened to inspire your brothers to evolve as well.

Change, and challenge, in this way is healthy and natural. It's natural to allow yourself to change as you age and learn. It is also natural to help those around you shed beliefs that they don't realize are limiting their capacity to care for themselves and others with more depth, connection, and understanding.

Build Healthy Romantic Relationships

We crave human connection. Relationships, at times, can either be a safe haven and sanctuary, or unbalanced spaces from which we feel the need to run away. This is especially true for romantic relationships, as they are some of the most complex relationships we encounter throughout our lives. In order to build healthy and meaningful romantic relationships, we have to allow our hearts to touch and be touched, and allow ourselves to receive the physical tenderness that brings comfort to the body. For these relationships to endure for whatever season they are intended, they need vulnerability and sharing from all parties involved.

MEDITATION: I AM CULTIVATING HEALTHY RELATIONSHIPS THROUGH INTERDEPENDENCE.

Human beings are social creatures. This means that we are hardwired for social connection. It is suggested that in the early days of our creation, social connections and sharing was how the human species survived. Early humans needed one another. Those closest to us helped sound alarms and ward off potential threats. Over time these relationships evolved into families, communities, and so on. Existing alongside one another was an evolutionary benefit, contributing to the group's survival.

As we have evolved, so have our relationships. While we are now, generally speaking, shielded from danger within the walls of our homes, relationships look very different than they did for our foreparents. We are not only called to simply exist alongside one another. We are learning to truly be with one another meaningfully, and not just for survival or propagation but out of choice. We choose spouses and partners to create a new form of family. This kind of relationship requires us, especially as Black men, to evolve. Romantic relationships today require us to exist on the spectrum of interdependence, or mutually dependent bonds.

Nature provides us with a helpful perspective on interdependence. The different parts of the world (the sun, the soil, the plants, the trees, etc.) collaborate in a complicated ecosystem that helps one another survive and thrive. These parts must work in tandem. Any disruption to the sunlight will negatively impact trees and crops. This will also impact the birds and insects that feed and help those crops flourish, and so forth. Sometimes, as human beings, we can forget that interdependence and connection are the methods by which we can survive and become our best selves.

For Black men in particular, this means operating in a way that wasn't modeled well for us. Black folks have been subjected to colonial thought across the globe, which has informed the hierarchal nature of men and women, children and families. An authoritarian father, for example, may rule a home in such a way that his word is law. He may be low on offering meaningful emotional responses and contact with his partner and children. Instead, he opts for only providing financial security and protection. But in this kind of relationship, there is a lack of balance. This throws the ecosystem out of whack, creating problems in the family ecosystem that cause cracks that turn into rifts and deep chasms as family members grow apart and move throughout time. This is true whether you are a family of four or a family made up of two partners who are building a life together. This kind of leadership style also does not meet the needs of the man, leaving little to no room for emotional support or physical co-regulation, and only reinforcing feelings of isolation and pressure to make all the right choices at the right times. Interdependence means understanding what the current relational environment requires from you and learning additional skills for your relational toolbox.

You can take lessons from the earth's system of interdependence to strengthen your romantic relationship. Take a moment to meditate on the lessons you could take from nature and its dynamic exchange of providing care and embracing collaboration. Can you allow yourself to be physically soothed and held as much as you soothe or hold your partner? Will you allow yourself to rest, be cared for and provided for too? If you are the fire in one moment, then your partner can be the water. At other times you may need to be the water, and your partner the fire. When you are down and struggling, you are the soil and your partner is the rain to help nourish you, and vice versa. With any relationship, whether it be between people or with the earth itself, mutuality and interdependence are the tools that help sustain a meaningful, healthy relationship.

Establish Healthy Boundaries with Family

We do not choose our families; we are born into them. At times, we may consider ourselves fortunate to come from where we do, and at other times our feelings may be more complex. Our feelings around family can lead us to create boundaries that we feel are necessary in order to maintain a sense of wellness. It is important to remember that when it comes to family, we do have agency in how we maintain the connections.

MEDITATION: I GIVE MYSELF PERMISSION TO HAVE BOUNDARIES WITH FAMILY THAT ARE HEALTHIER FOR ME.

How often have you heard some form of the phrase, "But that's your family!"? At this point, it should be considered a Black proverb. On one hand, this phrase can be well intended and encourage you to remember that familial relationships are special and deserve a lot of thoughtfulness. On the other hand, particularly in Black families, this phrase is often used as a way to diffuse disagreements, cast off conflict, and squash necessary boundaries or limitations. But this phrase, and the meaning behind it, need not be a fatalistic view you have of your family relationships. You always have agency and choice in how you engage, even if you aren't entirely convinced of it yourself.

There can be a lot of pressure on Black folks, and particularly Black men, to keep the peace among family members. But a family system in which someone is often taught to keep their grievances quiet, or to acquiesce due to fear of someone else's unreasonable behavior, is not a healthy family system. It is a system riddled with stress and dysregulated bodies and nervous systems. This can be tough to recognize when you are told that your deference to family members, particularly your elders, who may be the source of strain and tension, is not only essential but is your role. But when you internalize this message, and work to keep the peace within your family when you know that some things are wrong and harmful, you subject yourself and others around you to unnecessary stress and harm. You've likely felt the way your body tenses and changes when in this kind of family environment. Conversely, you may also recognize how your body relaxes, and your breath deepens, when you've left the stressful environment. Boundaries will keep you healthier. While there is no perfect or definitive line between prioritizing respect and holding healthy boundaries, this does not mean that having some limitations or standards is disrespectful or wrong.

In Black families, however, having some limits can be seen as a betrayal or sign of disrespect. In some cases, there is nothing you can do to convince a stubborn person otherwise. But healthier boundaries within a family are possible. This often comes with a lot of internal exploration of what you think you need in a relationship with a family member, and what your limits are in exercising that boundary.

This meditation can be an opportunity for you to offer yourself the space you need to determine what relationships within your family need attention. As you contemplate the relationships in your life now, give yourself permission to consider any points of pain or physical tension you've felt recently. Reflect on any patterns that have made you feel uncomfortable or angry. There may be some more vulnerable emotions here too, such as sadness or embarrassment. If these are coming up for you, remember that being mindful of yourself gives you the permission to sit with compassion and not judgment of yourself, no matter how intense these feelings may be. You can take a breath and remind yourself that being in touch with these parts of yourself is healing and necessary as you explore how you want to engage with family moving forward.

Unfortunately, many have internalized the idea that Black families cannot be tender and soft with one another. You may fear that this softness, especially for Black men and boys, will subject you to undue harm and victimhood in your life. But there is a balance between promoting resilience and being the first person to bully, or invalidate, a Black boy's (and man's) experience. You deserve to have family relationships that feel safe. You deserve to have relationships with family members and elders in which there is mutual respect and care, and you have the right to help craft the relationships that work better for you.

You deserve to have relationships with family members and elders in which there is mutual respect and care, and you have the right to help craft the relationships that work better for you.

Strengthen Connections with Family

There comes a time in every Black man's life when he starts to recognize that he has the most agency and responsibility over his own fate. As we grow and mature, we move from seeing our life circumstances as the result of decisions that someone else made and imparted on us, to seeing our own role in the life we lead moving forward. Part of the discovery in this period of revelation in life is learning how to intentionally choose to be in relationship with family and strengthen the relationships that are most important to you.

MEDITATION: I HONOR MY TRUTH IN SERVICE OF STRONGER CONNECTIONS WITH FAMILY.

Black families are spectacular in the ways we've been able to cultivate a sense of duty and responsibility to one another. This is, in part, due to the challenges we've faced in modern history. Surviving the horrors of enslavement, colonialism, and modern-day fascism and racism has helped reinforce the need to lean on each other in meaningful ways. Community provides us all with a safe haven. But due to relocation or physical distance, or emotional distance due to family issues or different perspectives on life, disconnection is also more prominent than ever. We crave meaningful connection within family and community, but we still struggle to invest in and sustain these important relationships.

Many of the challenges related to having strong familial connections rest with the differences in expectations and the challenges in being authentic with one another. Every culture, and family, has it norms. But as you may have noticed as you aged and began to create a life that is more aligned for you (and maybe even your new family), there is more opportunity for tension between what works well for you and what is expected of you from the family in which you were born. This difference can lead to a lot of tension, stress, and undesired distance. It may even lead to not feeling physically comfortable when sharing a space with family and always looking for an exit. In order to strengthen family ties, it's important to reflect on what can help you feel more comfortable and at ease.

More ease starts with being honest about the time you spend with family. Reflect on what that's been like for you lately. Have you been spending too much or too little face-to-face time with your family? Do you have the physical affection or proximity that helps you feel close and connected? Or is there something that you can learn about the quality of the time you spend together that requires some change? What do you need to feel more connected and comfortable?

As you start to explore these questions, your mind may start to offer up some answers and clarity, but it may also be challenging you to "do right" and follow the scripts that you've always held about your family relationships. This is where you can use the skill of the body scan to mindfully reflect on your deeper feelings and needs. As you ask yourself these questions, your body and intuition may more accurately highlight what feels right for you. Do a quick scan of your body, from head to toe. As you reflect on these questions, have you started to feel more stressed and has your breathing quickened? Have you noticed any increased tension or discomfort? Or, conversely, have your shoulders fallen and your breath deepened? Your body may start to relax as you get clearer on what could help you feel more connected and closer with your family. While the truth isn't always easy to acknowledge, the body seems to gradually ease when you are more authentic and speak your truth.

One of the strengths of mindfulness meditation is that it helps you connect with your deepest truths with less judgment and more compassion. When it comes to complicated ideas, like family relationships, mindfulness help you tap into your body as an additional resource to gain clarity and embody truth. This meditation is your permission to embrace your agency to make the changes needed to strengthen the connections you want with family.

Learn to Forgive Others and Embrace Release

As Black men, it is not often that we allow ourselves to acknowledge our emotional pain. The challenges we face to honor our feelings lie in the internalized messages we have about our own strength and vulnerability. But once we do acknowledge the harm we've faced at someone else's hand, how do we then approach forgiveness? In the space of mindful meditation we can learn to acknowledge the truth of our pain, accept its impact, and create the capacity to release the tension associated with our pain.

MEDITATION: I CAN FORGIVE AND MOVE FORWARD WITH LESSONS LEARNED.

Many of us struggle with the concept of forgiveness. On one hand, forgiveness requires that we first acknowledge the pain to ourselves. The pain itself can be devastating not just on the mind but also the body. Much of our chronic pain, digestive distress, restlessness, and tension can be caused, or worsened, by the harm we face from others. Forgiveness can be incredibly difficult, but it also an important way in which we heal ourselves. We don't have to forget or minimize our pain to gift ourselves the catharsis that forgiveness can provide.

It is difficult to seek forgiveness when the story we've long told ourselves is that we are invincible and unbothered by the wounding that can happen in relationships. Acknowledging our pain is the first, very vulnerable step. And often, we must contend with the shame of feeling in order to create space for any next steps. Instead, we often become avoidant and aloof, unintentionally robbing ourselves of the catharsis and resolution that can come with forgiving.

This cool, unaffected posturing has long been held by Black folks in the West, particularly Black men. Whether stoicism predates the enslavement of Black folks in the West is unclear, but there are countless stories of how swallowing our pain without so much as a wince was necessary. Enslaved Black folks had to cope through the horrors of dehumanization and violence to survive. As part of this survival, our ancestors had to keep quiet about their pain, at times even to themselves. Remnants of those survival skills can be seen in the conversations with Black men and folks across the modern diaspora. We have learned that to be strong and survive is to ignore our pain. We don't allow ourselves to bend, in large part, because of an unconscious recognition of our emotional fragility. We think that if we bend, we may also break. But to mindfully embrace forgiveness and freedom from the pain persisting in our bodies, we must first recognize the pain.

Nature often provides the blueprint for growth and healing, and the life cycle of the lotus flower reflects how something beautiful can come from challenging circumstances. In the beginning stages of its life, the lotus is nothing but a bud that germinates under water, deep in mud. It is dark and wet, with seemingly no sunlight to help it flourish. But somehow as the cold weather starts to turn warm, the buds of the flower continue to grow and ultimately rise to the water's surface. The bud blooms above water, in the sunlight, revealing its unexpected beauty despite its dark and muddy origins. The lotus is often thought of as a symbol of growth and a reflection on the themes of hardship and resilience. In this way, the lotus provides an analogy of how you can also explore the theme of forgiveness. The lotus does not forget from where it came: Its challenging beginnings are but a natural part of its story toward its growth and beauty. The same can be said about approaching forgiveness without forgetting.

Forgiveness does not mean ignoring that the pain and darkness (mud) existed in the first place; forgiveness is taking the opportunity to allow something beautiful to grow from periods of darkness. You can approach forgiveness with this same perspective; if life hands you pain and darkness, you can seize the opportunity to make something beautiful grow, like forgiveness (the blooming of a lotus). As you reflect on the pain you've experienced and work toward forgiveness, you are giving yourself the release that your body needs. As you take your next breath, repeat this meditation back to yourself: "I can forgive and move forward with lessons learned." Repeat this to yourself a few more times. On each exhale, allow your breath to release any tension you've held on to.

You can always make the choice to try and move forward, having sprung from the mud, and create something beautiful, just like the story of the lotus. Growth and catharsis do not happen without the submersion in darkness; they happen because of it. The same can be true for you if you so choose.

Align Your Values and Actions

When we are not operating in a position of alignment, our bodies can feel weighed down and like everything requires too much energy, time, and resources to manifest. When we are able to match our values and physical actions, we can find a sense of balance that is sustainable, and even capable of great growth.

**MEDITATION: WHEN I MOVE IN ALIGNMENT,
I INVITE MORE CONSISTENCY AND EASE.**

It's not at all uncommon for us to struggle with finding alignment between our values and actions. This is especially true when there are many external factors all screaming at us at once, causing a sense of confusion and chaos that's hard to overcome. This may resonate particularly with those of us who come from a family or community that has stakes in the game. In our actions and choices, these people are depending on us to do the right thing. Doing "the right thing" may have significant consequences for their life too.

As discussed in earlier meditations, this dynamic can create a great amount of pressure for anyone. This is especially challenging for Black men, as we are often unable to see ourselves as individual beings in the world. We are connected to family and culture in ways that leave us feeling responsible not only for ourselves, but for the collective perception. This sense of duty and responsibility can be clarifying, but only if our own voice is a meaningful part of the chorus of other perspectives and messages about our lives. All these voices and messages must exist in some sense of balance that feels right for the individual. It must be so to encourage inspiration over obliteration under pressure.

Values represent ideals and perspectives on what a person finds most important in life. For you, your value may be primarily in financial success or building a healthy family environment. Others might prioritize value in reaching certain professional achievements or contributing to the wider community. Your actions are how you embody your values in the real world. Your actions can be the long hours you put into work, or going to couples therapy to support your relationship. They might look like undertaking ongoing professional development or creating drives to provide resources for the community. When both your values and your actions are in alignment, you can feel empowered, energized, and in balance. When they are not, you may be confused and disoriented. This confusion leads to working too hard in ways that don't ultimately serve those value-based goals and that can take a toll on your physical (and mental) health.

Values and actions must exist in a healthy interdependent relationship for you to see the fruits of your labor. When you are acting in ways that you think are feeding your values but don't allow you to feel at ease, that is the moment to practice self-reflection and consider if there are other ideas or values that are complicating the picture. Once you have more clarity on those competing interests, then you can troubleshoot and determine what steps are necessary to find balance.

For inspiration, this meditation invites you to consider the interdependent relationship of the life cycle for plants. At first, a seed finds its place in the soil. Given that it is in the right environment, it needs two more main ingredients to succeed; it needs the power and light of the sun, and it needs the nourishment of water to flourish. When these two, the sun and water, are in alignment, that seed's buds ultimately bloom. The balance between these needs ensures its success and growth. When there is too much of one, and not enough of the other, the plant's survival is questionable.

Your personal values are the water and the sun of your actions. When they exist in relative balance, you create the conditions for your success. Take this metaphor as an invitation to consider whether your values and actions are currently aligned. If not, reflect on which you need more of to get back on the path toward alignment and success.

Allow Permission to Rest

Both the body and mind are in a constant state of awareness. Whether we are conscious of its impact or not, we are always reacting to the world around us, and our body's systems are constantly stimulated. Learning to fully embrace rest helps provide us with the rest our bodies need.

MEDITATION: I AM LEARNING TO ALLOW MYSELF TO REST WITH LESS GUILT.

Throughout the reflections in this book so far, you may have started to notice one of the most prevalent themes for Black men today: pressure. We are under a tremendous amount of pressure all the time, and yet as Black men we often don't allow ourselves to acknowledge it. We can also be oblivious to its impact on us. While each of our experiences with pressure is unique, it is critical to recognize how it shows up and the burden it places on us.

Pressure is hard to be mindful of because it is everywhere. We face pressures at work or school, from loved ones, and even from our community at times. The goals of being more successful, more responsible, and more enlightened are something we carry within us. As a result, we often may find it difficult to create space for physical rest. When we try to make that time, it can be hard to *feel* like we're resting too.

Take a moment to reflect on your experiences with rest. Have you ever sat down in your favorite chair with the goal of relaxing only to find your brain continuing to think of all the things on your to-do list? Have you experienced lying down for a nap only to find that your leg continues to shake, or you just can't manage to get comfortable? If so, you might be struggling with guilt associated with rest. Your body and your mind are likely having a hard time giving you the space to rest for the sake of giving your system a break. Guilt drives this difficulty.

No matter who you are or what you achieve in this life, you are deserving of rest. For all the pressures you face in your life, and even the accomplishments you create for yourself, you require moments of ease. You need to have opportunities in which you can absorb what it feels like to simply rest without expectation for anything else. The invitation here is to continue to challenge the thoughts and judgments that get in the way of giving yourself permission to rest. If you feel guilt, how can you begin to practice self-compassion in the conversations you have with yourself internally? If there is shame, consider what words of kindness you can start to build into your emotional vocabulary.

Rest is not a luxury. It is a physiological imperative. As the world around you continues to demand your attention and energy, give yourself the permission to spend moments in mindful breathing as you repeat this affirmation: "I am learning to allow myself to rest with less guilt." You deserve it.

PART 3

Spirit

Black men often have a complicated relationship with spirit. On one hand, Black folks are uniquely aware of how we are all connected to one another, often in ways that other communities find hard to understand. And on the other hand, as Black men we can sometimes struggle to feel deeply connected to our feelings and all things spiritual that are difficult to observe with our senses.

Rather than seeing evidence of its existence, spirit is often felt and experienced. Despite this, many of us hold the belief that spirit exists. This intuitive knowing and acceptance speaks to the origins of spirit and how it resides within us.

The origins of the word "spirit" are interesting, especially as it relates to the mindful practice of meditation. Derived from the Latin word "spiritus," "spirit" has been literally translated as "breath" or "air." This etymology not only references the invisibility of spirit to the eye, but additional translations also reference the ideas of life force, courage, and soul—ideas that are also intrinsically linked to Black men. It takes a tremendous amount of courage and strength to walk in this world as a Black man.

There is a force and energy that you as a Black man have access to if, and only if, you feed the connection to yourself, your community, and your spirituality. In a spiritual practice, you learn to make space for the unseen. As you practice connecting to the parts of your experiences that are unable to be seen by your eyes, or touched by your hands, you connect with a collective experience not limited by language.

In this part, you will find opportunities to connect with an aspect of yourself that you may not consciously access in everyday life. Here, you are invited to spend time with the feelings and internal experiences that are often unacknowledged. You are also invited to consider not only yourself, but what spirit offers in the context of your place in the greater sense of community and humanity. In these passages, you will find inspiration to focus on present centeredness and healing from spiritual and religious injury. The guidance and reminders in this part offer beacons of light along your spiritual journey of inner peace and self-discovery. Meet these meditations with an open heart as you discover what feels aligned and healing for you. Above all else, find peace of spirit in all that you encounter next.

Start by Connecting with Your Authentic Self

We live in a world where it is a challenge to be your authentic self. Black men are inundated with social rules and cultural expectations of who we're supposed to be and what we should find important in life. But through mindful self-reflection, you can start to learn and appreciate who you are on your own terms.

MEDITATION: I GIVE MYSELF PERMISSION TO EXPLORE MYSELF OUTSIDE OF THE EXPECTATIONS OF THE OUTSIDE WORLD.

From the moment our eyes open each day, many of us automatically reach for our phones and begin checking emails, reading the news, or catching up on social media. No matter where we look, we are forced to contend with what other people feel, think, or find important. And especially when it comes to online interactions, we're shown and told that we should find the same things interesting or worthy of our attention. All of this stimulation, directed by sophisticated algorithms, can make it difficult to pay attention to ourselves.

One of the core questions that you must face when starting to explore what it means to be your authentic self is to consider what it means to be truly authentic. Is your authentic self the one that has the internal thoughts you're afraid to share out loud? Or is your authentic self the person you most often show up in the world as, or the roles you embody as you navigate daily life? There is a case to be made that in some ways, all those examples comprise who you are as your authentic and complicated self. This meditation is an invitation to take an inside-out approach to learning to hold space for the person you are.

You can start to embrace your authentic self by spending some time in introspection and self-reflection. For example, rather than looking at any role or job you perform in life, take a step back and consider what it is you like about yourself. What traits, or characteristics, do you find feel central to you? Most often these traits have been a part of your makeup since you were young and have taken on a new color as you move throughout life and grow. What are the parts of you that you notice, appreciate, and maybe even love?

Next, take a moment to reflect on your beliefs and values. These kinds of ideas make up what is known as a "worldview" or your general perspective on the world. Beliefs and values are often the things you consider most important to embody in your life. Things like determination, honesty, or equality are some brief examples of core values. Simply put, what do you find most important, even if it doesn't meet the status quo of your external world?

Finally, take a moment to consider how much, or how little, you're able to express these parts of yourself to others. Do you find you're able to show your truest traits and characteristics to those around you? With the things you like about yourself, what barriers, if any, make it difficult for you to show and share those with others?

When you're trying to embrace your authentic self, it often takes a good amount of self-examination to better understand who you are, and what you find important, apart from the world's influence. While it can be a challenge to ask yourself these questions, this kind of contemplation helps you first acknowledge who you are on a soul level and then work toward embodying this version of yourself irrespective of the judgments of the outside world.

Black men deserve the self-awareness and acceptance that the world often tries to dictate. Your sense of self, and your spirit, is the unique combination of your ideas, values, and traits. Ultimately, you decide who you are and how you want to share yourself with the people around you.

Reaffirm Your Worth in Every Space

How can Black men see ourselves as worthy, when we're provided with so many reminders of the work we must do to be seen as valuable? Simultaneously, within us is a natural desire to come home to ourselves and experience true self-acceptance no matter the environments we are forced to navigate. By tuning into the practice of self-compassion, we can learn to settle our spirits and find worth no matter the challenging spaces we find ourselves in.

MEDITATION: I AM LEARNING TO ACCEPT MY WORTH THROUGH PRESENCE AND SELF-COMPASSION.

What does it mean to be a "high-value man?" If you've spent any time online in recent years, you've likely come across some content about what it means to be a man of high value. The truth is, the answer is subjective. Our value can't be found in a hot-take video online. The answer lies within each of us.

Of course, every Black man wants to be seen as worthy and valuable to the people he desires attention and affection from. There is nothing wrong with that. But unfortunately, when we are exploring that question, it also means that our worth is only determined by how someone else might see us. That sense of worth is external to us and subject to ebb and flow in different environments, and with different audiences. We can spend a lot of time chasing that information and comparing ourselves to the brothers around us who may be taller or have more money or something else that society has deemed makes them more worthy of attention and admiration. We forget that to experience a stable sense of self-worth we must begin with ourselves.

It's not a shame to have a sense of earthly ambition or desire to live up to some of the culture's standards of success. But when you spend time in deep exploration of yourself, you learn that worth is actually defined by the relationship you have with your own spirit. When you have a hard time seeing yourself through loving, compassionate eyes, the world's view on you can be a welcome distraction for superficial ways to find peace.

A deep sense of self-worth is not given by some outside source or Internet video, but it is intentionally cultivated by the practice of self-compassion. In what ways are you affirming who you are when you're taking on a new task? What kinds of compassionate thoughts do you practice when you notice you're comparing yourself to others in a professional space? Can you start to invest in the belief that the fact you are here means you are worthy, whole, and complete just as you are? This meditation is your challenge and your opportunity to affirm yourself in the here and now without qualification or expectation. How will you begin?

Define the Sacred on Your Own Terms

In our search for meaning, we sometimes seek spirituality for insight or refuge. Spirituality offers us a foundation upon which we grow and learn how to connect with ourselves and a higher power. However, we often inherit definitions of what is sacred in the universe and how we're supposed to apply spiritual learnings to daily living. Learning to discover our own personal relationship with what is sacred is crucial in sustaining a connection that has deep personal meaning.

MEDITATION: MY SPIRITUAL PATH IS MY OWN.

Black folks, especially in the West, are known for our spiritual and religious influences. Most Black families have within them a parent, most often a matriarch, that is highly invested in the spiritual lives of the family. When we are young, we inherit the stories and connections our families have with the sacred, whether that be a general sense of our space in the universe or a specific religious doctrine that influences the ways we should think and act to be worthy of salvation.

At times you may have felt some tension between your thoughts and opinions on religion and spirituality as you aged versus those of the people around you. It's not uncommon for older children, teens, and young adults to question the belief systems in which they were raised. Others start to explore their beliefs as they age and gain more life experience. Questioning is a natural evolution of a growing mind. Unfortunately, these investigations of the family's beliefs aren't always tolerated or welcomed. As such, we may find ourselves rejecting our family's sense of faith or surrendering to it altogether, never to question it again.

It's widely known that most people's sense of spiritualty and religion is off limits for interrogation. This is often because when we investigate and explore these ideas alongside others, we are met with the expectation of needing to justify or convince someone else that what we believe is right and true. Conversations around spirituality, whether within family or otherwise, have an unspoken agenda to persuade or convince. We often must contend with someone else's investment into our relationship with what we consider sacred. But what if your relationship with religion, or spirituality, wasn't governed by the need to fit into someone else's predetermined mold or convince them of something? How would you define what is sacred then?

Mindfulness provides an opportunity to look at yourself, and your thoughts, with less judgment and critique. When you practice a sense of presence without any other agenda than simply observing, you can feel relief from the pressures of fitting into a role that has been laid out for you or how you should define spirituality. Your definition of what is most sacred is up to you to determine. Use this meditation to question what is most sacred and true for you, without external pressures. What may arrive may be new or unnerving, but try to resist the urge to cast it away or judge it. Allow mindfulness to help you give it presence so you can truly listen. From there, you may begin to redefine what "sacred" means to you.

Make Meaning of Your Life

Life brings about its high moments and challenges, each carrying profound impact and consequences. But the stories we make of our experiences, and the insights we glean from them, are truly what help make our lives rich with meaning. This meditation will help you begin to make meaning of your life experiences and find healing.

MEDITATION: MEANING-MAKING IS MY PATHWAY TO SELF-DEFINITION AND HEALING.

As Black men, we often find ourselves in the unenviable position of other people telling our stories. Whether it's a media news item or a loved one close to us, when we lack the emotional vocabulary to talk about our lives and experiences accurately, other people become the authors of our stories. How do we begin to change that? We learn to embrace the power we have in making meaning of our experiences on our own terms. This starts with introspection.

To make meaning of our lives, we must first approach self-reflection with the intention to explore and discover without judgment. Introspection does present its challenges. When we take time to investigate ourselves and our past, we come face-to-face with some of life's pain. Some of this pain we've yet to move through and heal from. Introspection is especially tricky territory for Black men who may find it difficult to articulate not only the facts of our experiences, but also the impact on our spirits (as well as our bodies and minds).

Meaning-making helps you contextualize your life as an interwoven story. Think of meaning-making as a reflection on the different puzzle pieces of your life. The task is to place these pieces together, creating a foundation for how your experiences have impacted and shaped you. Meaning-making is not just what content is in the story, but how you perceive it and give voice to the content's meaning. This is helpful not only for reducing tension within, but it also empowers you to discover the language to translate these deeply personal stories to others. When you do, you can garner more empathy and understanding for yourself and solicit support from others.

Meaning-making is how you more deeply interpret the facts, or more observable parts of life. This meaning unconsciously inspires your behavior and choices. Devoting time to being mindful about exploring the meaning and consequences of your experiences empowers you through self-awareness. This insight is a powerful tool in creating an intentional, mindful life. For example, if you did well in school, you might be comfortable describing yourself as a smart person. But being "smart" might also hold other meaning than just making good grades. It may mean you walk into new academic or work settings with self-confidence as a default. Being smart may also mean you intellectualize your emotions rather than give yourself permission to embody them.

Rather than letting someone interpret your story, can you become the conscious author of your life's story and then share it with clarity and intention? If you do, you'll feel a great deal of compassion and ease waiting for you on the other side of the meaning you make.

Meaning-making helps you contextualize your life as an interwoven story.

Discover the Bells of Presence

When we start a practice of mindfulness, it can be difficult to find our footing. Settling into mindful awareness is a challenge, particularly when it's not yet woven into our daily lifestyle. Making the connection with the inner self becomes easier when we discover what spiritual leader Thich Nhat Hanh calls "the bells of presence."

MEDITATION: I DISCOVER THE ART OF PRACTICING PRESENCE BY OBSERVING THE WORLD AROUND ME.

Our minds are often quite busy during our daily lives. Most people have a variety of responsibilities to attend to and be conscious of. Vocations or professions come with their own pressures and stressors. We may also have a family to take care of, and relationships with friends and loved ones that require maintenance. When you add on the desire to achieve more, finding moments of inner peace to connect with your spirit is particularly difficult for Black men.

Whether you devote yourself to a practice of seated meditation in the traditional sense, or mindfulness during your daily activities, both require the capacity to connect to a sense of quiet. And when life all around you is fighting for your attention, then it can be hard to drop into a practice of grounding and connection. You must find reliable cues that help you pay attention to the immediate moment and environment around you to cultivate mindfulness. These cues and signals are the bells of presence.

In many forms of mindfulness meditation, the breath serves as a "bell" to connect to the present moment. When you focus on breathing deeply, you are drawing attention to what exists only in the present moment. This helps you connect with the self and divest from any distractions coming from the world around you. There are also other "bells" that help you slow down and pay attention. One way you can begin to discover which bells are most effective for you in connecting to mindfulness is to use any of your senses and notice what helps give you pause.

In walking meditation, for example, you are invited to pay attention to the sights around you. You may notice birds flying or other people walking. You're also invited to observe the sounds around you, such as idle chatter or the breeze blowing. You may notice the scents of the world and how the sun might feel on your skin, and so forth. These are cues, the bells of presence, that draw you into the moment and empower you to stay connected to the immediate environment. Having a cup of tea or coffee might be a bell of presence for you, just as much as a song or a book might help you slow down and practice being with yourself without the worry of whatever else may be going on outside of you.

Finding these signals that help you slow down and connect often takes some trial and error. Take a few moments now to consider when you feel most at peace—when your spirit feels at rest. Therein may lie some bells for you to integrate further in your mindfulness practice.

Acknowledge Your Faults

Often when we talk about personal development these days, it is a zero-sum game where we may find ourselves the losers in a rat race of glory and achievement. This primes us to see ourselves as either good or bad, perfect or faulty. But when armed with mindfulness, we can meet the self, and its perceived flaws, with kindness and consideration.

MEDITATION: I CAN ACKNOWLEDGE MY FAULTS AND LEARN TO ACCEPT MYSELF ALONGSIDE THEM.

Shame is one of the most powerful emotions that we experience as humans. And yet, it's not a feeling Black men talk about much, given how heavy and all-encompassing it can feel. To acknowledge that we are with shame only emboldens its presence—we think. However, the research tells us that shame thrives in silence, growing in the secrecy of the psyche and our spirit, tainting so many of our thoughts and feelings along the way. Many Black men struggle with the shame of not living up to an idealized version of ourselves. Rather than confronting it, we often suffer in silence, and ultimately, we unintentionally leak our shame through aggressive language or behaviors toward those closest to us. Mindfulness teaches us that we can be present with our perceived darkness and shame without continuous suffering.

For many of us, this shame stems from an upbringing in which our faults were met with harsh correction instead of kindness and compassion. It is of no surprise that often those same methods of feedback were also projected onto our mothers and fathers, their mothers and fathers, etc. Parenting is hard work, and it is an evergreen challenge to find the balance between compassion and correction. It is up to us, as grown Black men, to heal and offer ourselves the kindness necessary to see our mistakes or faults as things not to be punished or shamed, but viewed as inspiration for further self-compassion and growth.

Meditate on a recent time in which you made a mistake or got some feedback from someone whose opinion you trust. The critique likely stung and stayed with you. It's often the case that these moments evoke shame, leading to abusive self-critical thoughts about how unworthy or messed up you are. Now take a moment to consider how you might respond without as much self-judgment. What would that inner dialogue then sound like? If you had a loving caretaker, even the spirit of an ancestor with you, how might they help you see this pain point differently? How would they help guide you to new understanding?

For far too long so many of us have learned that shame is the great motivator for change. We're met with messages and advertisements daily that reinforce this message. But shame is not of spirit. Spirituality helps you see, and connect to, the deeper universal truth that you are worthy. You have the capacity to grow and become your best self, and spirit offers this insight through self-compassion.

Navigate Stereotypes and Microaggressions

The environment in which we live has a profound effect on the spiritual self. This part of ourselves is often subjected to the trauma and pain of racism, stereotyping, and microaggressions (the everyday slights and invalidations directed toward those marginalized by mainstream culture) that we absorb unconsciously. Even in a world marked by such harm, we have the power of choice in how we respond. As we tap into mindful awareness, not only can we name the harm, but we can also soothe and further protect the spiritual self.

MEDITATION: I HAVE AGENCY AND POWER IN CHOOSING HOW I RESPOND TO PAIN.

To be a Black man in the world means to exist despite the world's stereotypes and limitations. Every day in the media we see the long-held stereotypes that prevail about who we are and how we live, and judgments about the choices we make. The truth, as many of us within the community know, is far less dramatic. Black men are family men, providers, protectors, and more emotionally available than ever before. We positively contribute to our communities as parents, mentors, businessmen, and scholars, and yet mainstream stories about us seem stuck on highlighting the more challenging sides of the Black experience.

Unfortunately, these stereotypes are part of the inheritance of Black men from birth. Our caretakers, and other members of our community, may also internalize some of that same harmful messaging, creating a sense of pressure for us to compensate for the white gaze. We can't help but internalize bits of these messages. But with more awareness and intentionality, we can arm ourselves with spiritual (and mental) protection.

The first tool in resisting these tropes is mindful awareness. While you may know just how prevalent negative stereotypes are, how often do you allow yourself the ability to flag them as they happen? You may recognize them in the moment, but do you *notice* the impact on your spirit? When these stereotypes and microaggressions are quietly and effectively hurled at you in a work meeting or in some social gathering, are you able to practice mindfulness and understand that what you've just experienced is not just a racist quip but also a spiritual injury? Use this meditation to consider how often these injuries might happen, and how often you bypass the impact of them because of their normality. And as you move forward, practicing more awareness in the moment of these injuries, in and of itself, will be an act of spiritual protection.

Once you become aware of racialized injuries more in real time, you also discover what you need to recover from them. The awareness gives you power to appropriately assess the injury and decide what you need to heal or otherwise respond. At times, this may look like naming the injury for what it is and taking a moment to breathe so as to not internalize it. Other times you may temporarily remove yourself from the environment or even confront the aggressor. There are a variety of ways that you may choose to respond. It's up to you to determine what the moment requires of you.

When faced with attacks on the spirit, you can naturally seek to avoid the pain that comes with acknowledgment of the harm. But without acknowledgment or attention to your pain, there can be no healing. Giving yourself the power of presence provides the opportunity for you to recover and protect yourself from harm, which you are forever deserving.

Once you become aware of racialized injuries more in real time, you also discover what you need to recover from them. The awareness gives you power to appropriately assess the injury and decide what you need to heal or otherwise respond.

Embrace Creation and Collaboration

The modern world thrives on the principles of achievement and competition. This poses a risk to our spiritual health and the reality that success is best achieved through collaboration and interdependence. Otherwise, we are achieving only to destroy the competition. Peace and success can coexist if we allow it.

MEDITATION: WHEN I CREATE AND COLLABORATE WITHIN COMMUNITY, I INVEST IN MYSELF.

People like to say that men are naturally competitive. There is a biological basis for this, as the earliest versions of all humans needed to fight for limited resources. As such, survival at the time meant seeing any outsider as a threat. Unfortunately, we still operate socially and politically with a similar perspective—with the belief that in order to win at life, our brothers and sisters must suffer greatly. We do not have to accept this. One person's success and wealth does not necessitate another living as destitute.

Black men live at an interesting intersection of these principles of competitiveness and collaboration. On one hand, we understand that to achieve some sense of upward mobility in the mainstream world, we must adopt the competitiveness that thrives in those spaces. On the other hand, we also have deep recognition of the need for communal success as a people. We feel connected to our brothers and sisters within our communities. These contradictions create within us a tension that puts us continuously at odds spiritually.

You may have already experienced navigating the tension between striving for success to care for yourself and those closest to you, and risking the success of a peer. Sometimes your hand may be forced to make choices and take risks that create a loss for someone else. While there may be times when this choice is inevitable, this is always a spiritual injury.

The natural world provides a blueprint for the complex nature of collaboration and interdependence. On Mother Earth, when not overly subjected to the harm of man, ecosystems balance naturally. Each part or being has its own role to play. Each season has its benefits and disadvantages, its cycles of birth, death, and rebirth. When one part of that system suffers, so do the others. This is a message easily forgotten as a human on this Earth.

You are connected to the community and environment around you. When you ache, so does your brother. When your family suffers, so does another. This meditation isn't a mandate to change your entire way of living. Instead, it is an invitation to contemplate the ways in which you can further embrace the spirits of creation and collaboration in the immediate world around you. How can you continue to invest in the world in a way that is accessible and sustainable? Remember that when you do so, when you invest in the people in your community and society at large, you are also investing in yourself. You are creating in collaboration, honoring the ties that connect every person no matter where they come from or who they are.

Forge Your Own Path

How does one even begin to understand his own path? A life's journey has long been a topic of psychological and spiritual exploration throughout millennia. How to direct your life's journey is one of the most challenging questions you may explore. It requires rational thought and judgment, but also intuition and spiritual guidance to find a truly aligned path. In the earlier meditation, Own Your Story, you explored the concept of self-determination for your own life; here you are invited to further explore your life's journey with spirituality as your guide.

MEDITATION: I CONNECT WITH SPIRIT TO GUIDE ME ON MY PATH AND LIFE'S JOURNEY.

For many Black men, there is a sense of duty and obligation to not only consider ourselves, but also the lives of those around us as we determine our spiritual path. This isn't wrong; in fact, this consideration is necessary when we want to live thoughtfully and mindfully alongside others. After all, those closest to us have their own stakes and skin in the game in what happens with us. They are invested in what impacts us and them. This interdependence is healthy and inevitable. And yet, Black men must be careful to not allow someone else's idea of their path dictate their life's journey. Our paths may be informed by the desires and ideas of others, but ultimately these others do not have to live with the consequences of those choices. While they may be impacted, others in your life will never know your internal pain of living out of alignment with yourself. That is what makes it necessary to honor your needs and desires alongside your concern for others.

Who you are, and who you are destined to become, relies on your own idea of fate, spirit, and choice. And ultimately, you alone must live with the choices you make on this journey called life. In this meditation, create space for your private exploration of your life's journey. Take time to reflect on your past and the messages and choices of others that have guided your history. Once you've done so, then mindfully reflect on your own choices and actions that have gotten you to where you are today. Consider how your personal sense of spirituality has, or has not, contributed. Resist the urge to meet these moments with judgment and instead try to meet them with compassion. Look at these choices as puzzle pieces that have laid the brickwork for your path so far. Then, consider what choices you must still make and how each action can help you build a life that continually feels spiritually aligned and fulfilling for you.

No man walks through this world alone. And yet, as an individual, you are tasked with creating a life and a path of your own choosing. When you're able to devote time to mindful contemplation, you arm yourself with the spiritual guidance and intuition necessary to manifest the journey before you. You are deserving of the agency and choice in laying this path before you, no matter where you've come from or what may stand in your way. Your path is your own.

Acknowledge Your Grief

Healing is a complicated and continuous act, especially when the environment in which your live continues to expose you to the trauma and harm of racism. In mindful awareness, you can make space for this pain and find sanctuary in the spirit of healing.

MEDITATION: IN MINDFULNESS, I CREATE A SPIRITUAL CONTAINER FOR MY GRIEF.

To live in this world as a Black man means to be intimately familiar with the pain of being treated and seen as less than. Despite all the strides of justice and equality we have made, Black folks are continually subjected to the trauma of racism. All the while, we still strive for a place in the world that is fulfilling. The legacy of Blackness is an incredible testament to our collective resilience.

Black men are often taught that to be successful and healthy in this world we are to act as if we are invincible. We are taught to believe that it is our birthright to remember that we are forged in strength and iron. We are not often reminded that our spirits are also forged in tenderness and warmth. We are not reminded that every Black man was once a Black boy striving to make sense of a world that harmed his mother and father. That Black boy has turned into a Black man still striving to make sense of the horrors of Jim Crow, of the enslavement of his ancestors, and of the continual violence faced in carceral systems across the world. This is the grief and pain he carries, all while still being subjected to some of the same horrors himself.

There is not a spiritual or meditative practice that allows us to fully escape from the realities of the world. Unfortunately, we are only allowed brief respites from these challenges until the world truly becomes just. But this does not mean that taking these moments to honor our feelings of grief, and allowing them to wash over us, is futile. No, these moments are vital to the spirit. The moments of mindful awareness where Black men acknowledge our pain and grief are places where we can allow ourselves to heal and be held in presence. These are moments in which we can lay down our armor, and give ourselves the permission to grieve, rather than continuing the fight for our survival.

Facing deeper feelings, like sadness and grief, can feel daunting, especially if you've ever suffered through episodes of depression that you feared may not end. Know that when you intentionally meet these experiences with the support of spirit, they are not meant to be feared, only acknowledged and felt. When you give yourself the freedom to acknowledge your grief and create a spiritual container for it, you also provide the opportunity for catharsis. Within this space of acknowledgment and acceptance, grief and sadness start to shrink in relief. The sanctuary of mindful awareness can be the container for these feelings when they may seem overwhelming to face otherwise.

The moments of mindful awareness where Black men acknowledge our pain are places where we can allow ourselves to heal and be held in presence.

Reclaim Black Cultural Identity

One of the most unfortunate outcomes of the enslavement of African people in the West was the forced disconnection from Africa. The forced physical migration led to a spiritual and cultural disconnect. However, mindfulness allows us to rebuild and reclaim our cultural identity over time.

MEDITATION: IN RECLAIMING MY CULTURE, I RECLAIM MYSELF.

When our ancestors were brought to what is now known as the United States, they were not only subjected to horrific physical violence but also religious and spiritual warfare. Survival was often predicated on the acceptance of the Protestant religion, forcing an unimaginable choice. The mandate was to give all you are and have been, to be what enslavers said you must be, if you want even a chance of survival. Even with some of this loss of identity, our ancestors still found a way to keep some traditions and perspectives intact. These messages are hidden in stories shared in words, through the embodiment of our souls' rhythmical sways, and other practices unseen by white enslavers. These were acts of resistance, and the persistence of these cultural practices and understandings, often preverbal, are proof of a reclamation of heritage and pride in the legacy of Blackness.

Black folks have continued to find ways to socially and spiritually reclaim cultural identity. Now, maybe more than ever, Black folks are invested in tracing their lineages and learning the stories of their foreparents as far back as they're able. DNA analysis allows us to see the roots of our cells in the continent of Africa. TV shows, books, and movies continue to inspire, educate, and bring us back home to ourselves through education and entertainment. In all these things, we can experience pride and transformation through a loving gaze on Blackness. These are some brief examples of ways that we can reclaim parts of ourselves that are often left out of history books and museums that supposedly capture the "American" experience.

Reclaiming Black cultural identity begins with the realization that something, or some parts, have been lost or kept from you, due to the interminable whitewashing of history. You can choose to manifest reclamation in several ways, such as learning more about the history of Black folks in America and throughout the world. Reclamation may also look like celebrating the achievements of Black folks throughout the diaspora or addressing misinformation whenever you come across it. All these acts are revolutionary when Blackness is under constant scrutiny and attack. The harmful rhetoric and politization of white supremacy into law (again) threatens the spiritual (as well as physical and psychological) health of Black men and communities. Investing in cultural reclamation is protection and affirmation of all that you are, and the heritage that enlivens your spirit, as well as your mind and body.

Embracing Black cultural identity is not about acknowledging struggle, but more so creating space to experience the fullness of Blackness in all its forms. Blackness is everything, and when you're able to create space to connect to it, you realize that so are you.

Explore Intersectionality

We live in a world in which we are continuously made to evaluate ourselves against others. Most of this takes place online as we scroll our news feeds mindlessly. Harmful and bigoted rhetoric often reaffirms our fears and anxieties about ourselves and those who seem different from us. These divisions, in the eyes of spirit, are inconsequential. By exploring intersectionality (the privileges or oppressions we experience based on our overlapping identities), Black men can drop the harms of division and learn to practice peace with the community and culture at large.

MEDITATION: I SEND PEACE TO ALL MEMBERS OF MY GLOBAL COMMUNITY.

The systems of racism, patriarchy, and homophobia make us pawns in the greater game of capitalism. Its competitive nature plays on our deepest concerns and puts us at odds with one another. These systems highlight and manipulate our differences to keep us busy with the distraction of competition. This keeps us from seeing how all of us, no matter our differences, are all negatively impacted by the systems. By constantly seeing other members of the global community as "the others" we forget we are all more alike than we are different. By acknowledging the spirit of interconnection that exists between us we can craft a planet that is more equitable and sustainable for everyone.

Turn on the news on any given day and you will see how we are told to think about women, disabled folks, immigrants, and members of the LGBTQIA communities. The message from the harmful majority is, "If they are getting something, then you're losing something. You better make sure they don't get the special treatment YOU deserve." As we scramble for any semblance of power and control in our lives, we can easily become lost in this narrative. In a quest for a more just society and the equality we feel is deserved, we can find ourselves motivated by lust for power. When subjected to this kind of programming repeatedly, it becomes easy to see any other person as a threat to our success and value in the world.

This division exploits our evolutionary tendency to seek out safety from "the other" or someone who we don't recognize as part of our own close-knit community. They, instead, become competition subject to ridicule and sacrifice. This ignores the reality that we, as members of the global majority, are more alike than we are different. Through acts of solidarity and intentional communal care (such as advocacy, activism, and community resource programs, etc.), we can operate in a way that is much more spiritually aligned than fighting endlessly for scarce resources, whether they are concrete like financial resources, or more abstract like psychological acceptance.

You don't have to continue to subscribe to the ideals that encourage competition to the point of devaluing someone who is different. Difference also ignores the fact that none of us is one singular thing. We exist and live at intersections of identities. For example, some women are also Black. Some Black men are gay or bisexual. Some men are also disabled. There is no one right way to exist as a human. Extending care and compassion out to others who may exist in the world in different ways than you is a poignant exercise in spiritual universality.

When you are faced with the messages that pit you against other members of your global community, and when the message is meant to disparage or belittle them, practice the art of *metta*, a loving-kindness meditation. Instead of stoking the fire of division and competition even within yourself, offer yourself self-soothing through the words "May I be happy. May I be well. May I be safe." Then practice sending that same kindness out to friends, community members, and even strangers who might also need support. In this moment of reflection, send out that same loving-kindness you've just offered yourself. Say out loud, "May you be happy. May you be well. May you be safe. May you be peaceful and at ease." What you'll find is that when you practice loving-kindness with yourself more, it becomes easier to also extend this same healing energy outward, even to those who seem different from you. This practice is a reminder that while everyone may look different and may live life differently, each person wishes for the same sense of peace and safety. This meditation is a reminder that you, and everyone else, deserve it.

Create Inner Stillness

The world is a busy place and with that, it also encourages a busy spirit. With mindfulness, Black men are able to create a moment that allows for inner stillness. This practice is creating a place of refuge and sanctuary uncontrolled by outside chaos.

MEDITATION: WHERE THERE IS INNER STILLNESS, I FIND PEACE.

The world we live in can be incredibly demanding of our attention. Some of this attention and focus is directed toward things we find entertaining or interesting, while at other times it's also easy to find ourselves trapped in arguments and conflict. This unfortunately can keep us distracted from finding the refuge that we're so desperately looking for.

For Black men, stillness is critical for a couple of reasons: First, when we are out in the world, we are forced to contend with the stereotypes and judgments of others, which is exhausting. Even in our closest relationships, we may sometimes find ourselves performing, or playing into, stereotypes and expectations. In this performance, we lose sight of ourselves. Second, inner stillness helps Black men meaningfully invest in our innate capacity for healing. Learning to be with ourselves, and developing our own ability to nurture and heal, is part of our continual evolution. We can be healed by others and also take accountability for our own healing. Cultivating inner stillness is a practice of honoring the healing capacity that we have within.

This meditation is an invitation to imagine what inner stillness can feel like for you. Begin to envision what it would be like to spiritually exist in an experience not clouded by the chaos and noise of the outside world. With each breath, and within each moment, you are practicing the act of simply being with yourself and giving your spirit freedom from expectations, social norms, and pressures. In this moment you are meeting yourself with calmness and stillness. Here you experience an unburdening of all the ideas and things about the world that can sometimes feel burdensome and make you weary. Here is a place of refuge not just for the spirit, but also for the mind and body.

With no need to think or speak, and with no pressure to be anything other than you are, you are creating inner stillness. This moment is where you get to meet a version of yourself not tainted by the outside world. This is a space for you to heal. Take a moment to gather a large inhale and acknowledge what this moment feels like in your body. Notice the ease that begins to wash over your mind. Reflect on what this stillness does for your spirit. This is the experience of being.

The space of inner stillness is one that is always available to you. It's a moment, a place, and a time in which you can experience freedom from the world and perhaps even the sense of self you've forged out of necessity. This space is a space for being and not doing. Stillness is your sanctuary.

*Stillness is
your sanctuary.*

Celebrate Black Excellence

The stories we are fed about the Black experience become part of our legacy. Sometimes these are stories of survival, and other times, they are stories of profound inspiration and achievement. Whether we embrace and internalize or refute these stores, they become part of our cultural makeup. As we continue to move forward as a people, it's important to give more space and energy to the resilience, contributions, and creativity of Black folks.

MEDITATION: I HONOR AND CELEBRATE BLACK EXCELLENCE AND INVEST IN ITS ENDURING LEGACY OF GREATNESS.

It's hard not to see the Black experience only through the lens of challenge and oppression. Unfortunately, we have an abundance of examples of how Black folks have been made to suffer and struggle. One of the unfortunate byproducts of these stories is that we unconsciously internalize them and come to identify Blackness through sacrifice and struggle. These stories are necessary recollections of our cultural experience and should be honored. However, being able to see the legacy of our experience more fully can help us practice reverence for not only what our ancestors have survived and championed, but also the excellence that presently exists in the world around us, and even within ourselves.

When was the last time you dedicated time to reading about the incredible achievements of your foreparents? Veneration is the act of practicing meditation on and reverence for those who came before you: the ancestors that paved the way for you to be the man you are today. When you stop and reflect on their legacies, who are those leaders in the culture who created the ability for you to live and breathe as you are? What creative contributions and sacrifices did ancestors in your own family make that helped you get to where you are?

Additionally, who are the people in the present who move the culture forward? Whether in politics, the arts and entertainment, or academia, who can you celebrate for their creativity and contributions? Take a few moments to consider how these achievements motivate and guide you as you continue to make your way through this world. Similarly, consider the ways in which you, yourself, are excellent and contribute to the environment around you. How are you showing up in excellence and inspiring others to do the same? What are the ways that you can contribute to the continued evolution of Black men in this world? In what ways can you manifest excellence through your own behavior, or by investing in the excellence of others in the future?

Being a Black man in the world today often means facing continuous challenges and fighting for survival. But no matter the circumstances, you also thrive. Investing in your spiritual health means giving yourself the permission to acknowledge and invest in Black excellence in all its forms: past, present, and future. When you celebrate this, you honor all that is sacred and that which cannot be tainted by the world's limiting stories.

Create Space for the Unseen

Spirituality can be hard to define, as each individual has their own interpretation of what it means to them and their life. In this meditation, you are invited to use mindfulness as a tool to discover intangible sensations, intuition, and guidance that are often unseen. This is your opportunity to direct your attention to how spirit is a part of your life even if you have not been entirely conscious of it.

MEDITATION: I INVEST IN THE UNSEEN TO HONOR MY INHERENT SPIRITUALITY AND INTUITION.

When we explore mindfulness through the body, we utilize things like the breath and our other senses to observe the world around us. We tune into mindful breathing to bring about presence and relaxation, and we observe what we see and hear to stay present. This is how the body is a tool for practicing mindfulness. This is especially helpful for Black men who may struggle to embrace and practice introspection on a routine basis. The body connects us to our internal experience and allows us to connect with spirituality, which is often felt but rarely seen.

Spirit invites us as Black men to connect with internal feelings, intuition, and guidance from God, the universe, or our ancestors. Unlike body (and mind), these things are much harder to quantify or observe; thus, they present a challenge for our belief in their existence and usefulness in guiding our lives.

When you quiet the world, and invite in presence rather than just thought, you can connect to intuition rather than only logic. One is not better than the other, but connecting with your intuition can help you embrace the untapped spiritual guidance you have within you. When you have this sense of connection and awareness you are much less vulnerable to messages that prey on your insecurities and weaknesses to drive decision-making. When you make space for the unseen, you make connection with what is true for you, even if it is not easily described or visible. Spirit reminds you that it doesn't have to be visible for it to be real or true.

In this meditation, ask yourself a question. It could be about any topic that's important to you, whether it's relationships, work, or something else about your personal world. You may ask yourself something like, "Am I in the right relationship for me?" Or "How do I continue to grow and develop in my career?" Then take note of what immediately comes up. You'll likely notice the mind first, racing in with thoughts and solutions. You may also notice the body show up in reaction, with quickened breath or tension in your neck or body, or something else. Then, wait. As the discomfort or fear subsides, ask your question again and simply wait. Wait for the message to be driven into your gut. After a few moments, scan your body and see what sensations you notice, or if any thoughts unclouded by fear or worry arrive. Pay attention to this response and unseen answer as your intuitive knowing shows up for you. Even if the answer is challenging to accept, when it is informed by intuition, it won't feel fearful. Instead, you'll feel a sense of clarity and certainty. You may even feel resolute. This is the practice of creating space for the unseen.

Connect with Your Ancestors

Despite being more connected than ever before, people are feeling as isolated and disconnected as ever. Men in particular report unparalleled levels of isolation. While we continue to make space for others in our lives, our ancestors can also provide connection and safety from an otherwise adversarial world for Black men.

MEDITATION: I CONNECT WITH MY ANCESTORS TO CONNECT WITH MYSELF AND COMMUNITY.

Black men can invest in relationships with their ancestors to cure feelings of isolation and disconnection. So many of our stories in the West, in particular, exist in disparate fragments. Due to the Transatlantic Slave Trade and forced indoctrination of English and foreign religious traditions, so many of us don't feel deeply connected to our deepest roots. As a result, it can then be difficult to invest in relationships with the ancestors that feel real and connected. A spiritual practice of inviting in these relationships can offer us solace when we're in need of inspiration and support. This practice can bring about peace when our hearts and spirits are weary from the continual fight for equality and justice that has yet to be realized.

Use this meditation to connect with a long-past ancestor and reflect on the stories you have heard or read about them. For those of us without the stories of our ancestors long ago, it can be helpful to take a few moments and reflect on a living ancestor, such as an aunt, uncle, or grandparent, that you feel connected to. As you begin to reflect on what this person has meant to you individually, start to examine the scope of your focus expanding. Start to think of the role this person plays in your family. Think of their relationships with other family members, and then allow your imagination to venture into the time in which they came of age, with all its benefits and challenges. Perhaps you even have some shared family memories that come to your mind. These memories may bring about joy and happiness. They may also bring up grief and sadness. Allow yourself to sit with it all.

Reflect on this person's triumphs and celebrations. Envision the kinds of things they must have had to endure as your mind weaves together the history of your family. Allow yourself to envision the things this ancestor experienced, and how they made it through and persevered. All of this is part of your inheritance. These stories, images, and narratives of survival have been with you since the day you were born.

Imagine that this ancestor, and maybe many others before them, had hopes and dreams for you and your parents. Whether they were able to physically be present for your birth or not, know that as birth is given to any new generation, the entire family wishes for not only survival, but the continual progress that each generation brings. This ancestor, and all the ancestors that came before them, likely wished and prayed for you to become the man you are today. As the spirits of your ancestors live on, not constrained by physical time, they continue to conspire with all that's within your spirit so you can become the man that you are destined to be. These ancestors are always with you in spirit, praying and wishing that all they lived through and prepared for has been enough to allow the family legacy to continue and thrive.

When the pain of loneliness or the worries of the world make you doubt yourself and your resilience, remember that these ancestors are guiding you and instructing you through your dreams, your hopes, and your intuition. As you practice sitting in connection with these ancestors, you tap into their presence and resilience. Give yourself the freedom, and permission, to let them be a part of your story whenever you need them.

Find Your Sacred Space

We all need a safe space to be ourselves and lay down the armor of vigilance. Physical places of refuge are necessary, but so are spiritual and psychological spaces that allow Black men to be held by environments of comfort and security. We also need spiritually safe space to be at home with ourselves. This meditation will allow you to create and access a sacred spiritual place of your own.

MEDITATION: I GIVE MYSELF THE GIFT OF SAFETY IN THIS SACRED SPACE.

Just as our bodies and minds are the vessels that carry us throughout the world, so are our spirits. This more abstract aspect can be difficult to feel connected to if we are too focused on relying on what we can observe and touch and reason as our only reality. But how we see the deepest parts of ourselves, and the sense of spiritual connection we feel with the world around us, are important places to invest in our health and wellness too.

All too often, Black men are subjected to standards, fears, and obsessions about who we are and what we do (or are not allowed to do). We continuously gather data about where our presence is not welcomed or, at the very least, is challenged by dominant norms of whiteness that we can never actually live up to. Unfortunately, this creates a type of awareness and vigilance where it can be difficult to feel at peace. This vigilance is intensified when you are a Black man who doesn't fit the norms and expectations within the community as well. Finding sanctuary can be difficult. Mindfulness helps us create a space that provides for refuge from others' expectations and standards, even our own that exacerbate worry and pressure our health and wellness.

This meditation is an invitation for spiritual creation. As you reflect on the spaces in life that feel like they require some performance from you, allow yourself to now slow down and begin to imagine a space that offers you nothing but healing and protection. This place could be one for quiet reflection or somewhere that holds all your favorite things or memories—anything that brings you peace.

Start to envision what this environment looks like. As your eyes scan this place, you might see photos of loved ones or cherished memories from different times in your life. This space could be based on somewhere real that you've already visited or an entirely imagined location. It's a place you're creating in the here and now. As you contemplate this space, envision how it makes you feel.

Could this space bring you a sense of relief? Is it a place where you can pray or lay down your burdens without fear of someone else's judgment or evaluation? Could this space become a vault for worries and concerns that otherwise might seem hard to share with others in daily life? The goal of this sacred space is to provide for you just what you need. You do not need to feel worry, shame, or guilt for needing or creating this safe haven. We all need spaces that feel safe for us to unburden ourselves. This sacred space that you're creating right now is always available for you whenever you need it.

This sacred space you've just created is only for you to feel at ease. No one else has access to it, as it only exists in the realm of your spirit and imagination. The only thing you need to access it is a little bit of time and conscious intention to visit it.

When you feel the pressure of life begin to overwhelm you, or personal challenges keep nagging at your heart, remember that with a little bit of time, and a few conscious breaths, you can bring yourself back here. You can bring yourself back to this sacred space where you may rest without worry. This is a space you need and deserve.

We all need spaces that feel safe for us to unburden ourselves.

Revisit a Dream

When I was young, I was deeply inspired by Langston Hughes's poem "Harlem." This work, while brief in form, boasts powerful questions about what happens to us and our hopes and dreams. This poem grants implicit permission for Black folks to dream in challenging times. This meditation continues to invoke this permission as you begin to revisit your own dreams.

MEDITATION: I RECONNECT WITH MY DREAMS TO REDISCOVER MYSELF.

Black folks in the West have long been forced to dream about, and to seek out, a sense of spirit and beauty to visualize what has not been reflected in their daily lives. Dreaming of what could be offered freedom from what was. This kind of dreaming is still a collective hope and a wish that life has yet to gift us. Dreaming is necessary. On the other hand, dreaming has also been positioned by critics as an unrealistic privilege. After all, how can you dream when the capacity of your spirit (and mind) has been so challenged that the soul has forgotten that hoping is even possible? It's a valid argument, and while you may land on either side of this debate, meet this moment in seeing dreaming as a tool that helps you reconnect to your highest self.

Aside from the hope that dreaming can offer Black folks collectively, it is critical that Black men also offer ourselves the ability to revisit the dreams of our past. The world can be so hard on Black men. This harshness metabolizes in the spirit and beats the light out of many of our eyes. Even while young, the spirits of Black boys can be weary from carrying the weight and realities of the world. In carrying this burden, we lose sight of the beautiful boys we may have been before the world, or our families, beat the dreams out of us. And just as Hughes offered in "Harlem": What happens to those dreams? Where do they go and how do you continue to carry the grief of those lost dreams within?

This reflection offers you radical permission to not only answer those questions but to begin to explore what it could mean to bring those dreams back. If you were able to revisit the dreams of your childhood, what would these dreams tell you about who you were, and maybe still are?

Reclaiming parts of the self that have long been lost is a healing ritual for the spirit. When these pieces reunify, you get to experience an internal homecoming. When this happens as a Black man, you get to experience a sense of ease and an internal cohesion that can always exist within. Knowing who you are at your core, regardless of the challenges in embodying it, offers a gradual inclusion of these parts into your waking life over time. Every Black man deserves that.

Meet Your Inner Child

From the time that Black boys are brought into the world, they are often seen as older and stronger than they are. For Black men to embrace our fullest spiritual selves, we need a homecoming to the tender and more vulnerable parts of ourselves, the inner child. This meditation will help you meet your inner child and embrace him.

MEDITATION: I MEET MY INNER CHILD TO HEAL. I GIVE MYSELF PERMISSION TO MEET MY YOUNGER SELF WITH VULNERABILITY AND EASE.

If you pay close enough attention, you'll see how often young Black males are indoctrinated into becoming men long before their bodies do. It's common for families to refer to a young Black boy as "little man" and other nicknames that project onto him adultification. Black boys are often taught to take on qualities of manhood (strength, protection, being providers, etc.) long before they even come to understand themselves fully as boys. This premature aging robs Black men of normal boyhood.

Many parents do their best to create environments that protect Black boys. The community is in continuous conversation about how to best allow Black boys to fully preserve their innocence and simultaneously prepare them for the world that treats their skin color, textured hair, and full lips as indicators of difference, and even unworthiness. The intentions from many caregivers are pure, and yet they manifest a world in which Black boys are hyperaware of the ways in which they don't fit in mainstream spaces.

This adultification occurs not only in the context of race but also gender. Early messaging on gender often robs Black boys of the possibility to fully embody natural qualities like empathy and tenderness. We learn that the expiration date on these qualities is short. It is only appropriate to show up in the world in this way for the first few years of life. After that, this emotional availability becomes subject to many projections, besmirching young Black boys as "feminine" or somehow unworthy.

Reclaiming the inner child starts with giving yourself the permission to revisit the parts of yourself lost to this conditioning. Meeting the inner child may look like giving yourself permission to acknowledge your ability to feel. It may also look like learning to embrace play and the expressions of levity and joy, which are often thought of as youthful and feminine qualities. It may also look like learning to speak to the younger part of yourself with tenderness and kindness that may not have been part of your earliest years on this earth. Meeting the inner child in all these ways is a reclamation of power and spirit to which every Black man is entitled.

Whether well intentioned or malevolent, Black boys are often robbed of youth in this world. This meditation is your invitation to meet with this younger version of you and invite his influence in your life. Meeting him means practicing being in communication with the inner child in everyday life. With more presence in this connection, you'll be better equipped to honor your needs, and maintain relationships that are fulfilling to your spirit, as well as your mind.

Shed Internalized Harm

Embracing spirituality means embracing the ethereal through practice and study. For Black men, embracing spirituality also requires recognizing how a sense of self is often hijacked by mainstream ideas rooted in robbing Black folks of their humanity. Reclaiming your spirit relies on developing a greater sense of awareness of the harms perpetuated by racism and discrimination and developing the spiritual protection necessary to ward off internalized harm.

MEDITATION: WITH AWARENESS, SELF-COMPASSION, AND SPIRIT AS MY GUIDES, I SHED INTERNALIZED HARM AND EMBRACE HEALING.

Presence is an incredible gift. The practice of mindfulness gives us the tools to be present with ourselves and our thoughts and feelings. This sense of connection strengthens the relationship we have with ourselves and offers us sanctuary. It also provides the opportunity to transform pain and suffering through greater awareness and self-compassion. As we grow more aware of ourselves, and the impact of the environment around us, Black men become more attuned to the spiritual injuries we endure daily.

If we believe that life is suffering, then we also accept the premise that as we live, we experience injury. At times, these injuries we suffer come from the hands of another. In other moments, which is often the case with long-standing oppression and discrimination, we unconsciously become our own abusers, internally subjecting ourselves to the same harm our aggressors once inflicted upon us. However, when we draw mindful awareness to the inevitable internalizing harm, we start to shrink its influence. This is the power of mindfulness as a practice in spiritual healing.

Black men are subjected to a myriad of stereotypes and misinformation about who we are and our role in the world. These tropes, often bolstered by racist and otherwise harmful ideologies, find ways to burrow into our consciousness over time. As our ancestors continued to face opposition and colonialism, they were stripped of their culture, their religions, and a sense of self marked by pride and confidence. We collectively have already begun the process of unlearning some of the harmful messages forced upon us through colonization and spiritual subjugation. And yet, collectively and individually, we still have so much work to do to unpack these messages and move forward with less gunk burdening our spirit.

What does internalized harm look like? For Black men, this harm can look like endorsing or perpetuating colorism in ourselves and romantic partners. Internalized harm can look like still struggling with the size of our lips, the shapes of our noses, or a general preoccupation with what falls between our legs as the ultimate value of our sense of pride and manhood. It can look like struggling to free ourselves from the shackles of overworking and a desire to assimilate into white spaces despite the continuous signs of anti-Blackness.

The legacy of trauma based on race is intergenerational. As our parents, their parents, and their foreparents fought for physical survival, they also fought for their spiritual survival. And yet, some of these harmful messages about who Black men are, and who they're supposed to be, have slipped through the cracks. We still contend with these messages daily, even in moments we may no longer consciously recognize. Some of these ideas have become so widespread and ingrained that we've also internalized them as normal parts of our culture. What could that mean for our spiritual enduring throughout time?

In intentional moments of stillness you can investigate these themes in your own life. Supported by the intention of self-compassion you can meditate on the stories you inherit from others and discern whether or not their spiritual truths are also your spiritual truths. What has become yours, the suffering of harm that has been programmed into your spirit time and time again, is not a burden you are forced to continue carrying. You have the agency, and the spiritual fortitude, to investigate and challenge it. In the practice of examination, you ultimately can decide what principles feel aligned for you and what principles continue to perpetuate harm on your spirit. When your suffering becomes conscious, it is then a choice between continuing to accept the internalized harm or resisting it as baggage that is no longer yours.

Create Space for Joy As Resistance

A significant portion of our story as Black men is rooted in resistance, which is necessary to march toward our birthright as equal and whole beings living in the world. To continue to move forward in this pursuit of wholeness, we must also make room for joy. This is often easier said than done for Black men. Fortunately, this meditation offers some insights to help you meet this challenge.

MEDITATION: WHEN I MAKE SPACE FOR JOY, I MAKE SPACE FOR HEALING MY SPIRIT.

Joy is a powerful act of resistance. To meet the challenges of the world with joy in our souls, we recognize that beauty in this world is a balm for healing. Unfortunately, for many of us, being disconnected from the self, and our feelings, is a behavior we have learned as we've grown up. Black boys are often taught from a very young age that to be in touch with our feelings, and to express them, is something we should avoid. We lose touch with these beautiful parts of ourselves. With that, we lose the part of our emotional range that connects us to feelings like excitement and joy. We learn that to perform masculinity well, and to be accepted, joy must die with boyhood. Even still, that death often comes for us much too soon. It certainly comes earlier than it does for our white counterparts.

This internalized emotional limitation also protects us from feeling the depths of our challenges as well. Being cool and unaffected in this way helps us navigate the world's ills and vitriol. With time, we internalize this cool persona, and it robs our spirit of the experience of lightness, joy, happiness, and warmth. With the loss of innocence and internal emotional connection, we lose access to lightheartedness. And that lightness is important for the health of our spirit. As writer and scholar Audre Lorde suggests, levity and joy can provide the spirit with the "energy for change" needed to reconnect with feelings of hope and continue resistance in the face of harm and oppression.

It's time to harness your joy and make space for it. This meditation is an invitation for you to reflect on the moments, likely in early life, that you found to be joyous. What was a moment in childhood when you remember feeling unburdened by life's challenges or responsibilities? In which moments did your stomach and cheeks hurt from smiling and laughing for so long? How were you able to create a sense of adventure and awe in your life back then? Revisiting these memories helps you open a spiritual portal back to parts of yourself once lost or minimized to survive as a Black man in this world. Also reflect on how you will move forward creating intentional space for these kinds of feelings now, irrespective of your age and life responsibilities.

Whereas resilience enables you to continue to meet the necessary fight for your physical and psychological survival, joy is how you feed your spirit. This meditation is your invitation for curiosity in how you can bring joy to your spiritual self moving forward.

Joy is how you feed your spirit.

Trust the Unknown and Embrace Surrender

Life is full of uncertainty. Learning to engage with and manage the unknown is a skill fostered by our investment in the spirit and the universe—a universe that can never be entirely known. In this, you may find a lesson that there is also freedom in not knowing and learning to find yourself within surrendering to a reality that is out of your control (or even to a temporary setback).

MEDITATION: I GIVE MYSELF PERMISSION TO RELEASE THE PRESSURE OF KNOWING. WITH THIS, I LEARN TO SURRENDER.

As Black men, we can often get caught up in our resilience and power, and for good reason. These ideas are often taught to us as part of a legacy of survival that is passed down through generations. Our ancestors were survivors! This means that we should also be able to handle any challenges that come our way and overcome them. This is part of the legacy of our strength.

These are beautiful reflections on Blackness and are tenets we should never forget. Yet it is also important to remember that we are not always strong enough, nor smart enough, to respond to any situation with effective solutions. We cannot always fight through life with strength. Sometimes fighting for life means acknowledging that we've been knocked down and must accept the pain and confusion that comes with temporary defeat. We can learn to cultivate the power of discernment and surrender.

As Black men, we often arm ourselves with knowledge that we think can spare us from pain and discomfort. But we must learn to also accept losing a battle. The acceptance of loss and the confusion of defeat enable us to make peace with our limits as human beings. We do not always have the remedy or insight to resolve a situation. Sometimes we are incapable. This is not a character flaw; it's a spiritual truth that we must learn to accept in navigating life. We are not always able to respond and resolve. Sometimes the world, the spirit, or even God (however you may define that) has other plans. Letting go of the expectation that we can always have all the answers is an acknowledgment of the surrender.

With the pressure to show strength, knowledge, and resilience, the humanity of Black men is sometimes lost. You forget you are not always in control, nor do you have to be. You didn't learn how to tolerate uncertainty or embrace surrender. Then you try to fix as much as you can until the mind and body start to crumble. What if you didn't always have to have the answers or be strong? Could you still be a worthy man if you learned to surrender too?

These are reflections I invite you to sit with as you consider what it means to surrender as a Black man in this world. It's likely that you are not often offered the space to be vulnerable and humble as the world continues to challenge you at almost every turn, but can you begin to offer yourself the freedom of surrender?

Acknowledge Religious Harm

What do we do when the places that are meant to provide refuge harm us? We acknowledge the harm and begin the process of recovery, on our own terms. In this meditation, you'll reflect on the harms (spiritual, mental, or physical) faced within the realms of religion and spirituality.

MEDITATION: WHAT I NAME, I BEGIN TO HEAL.

For many Black folks across the diaspora, spirituality and religion play a significant part of our lives. Many of us have grown up in a religious tradition, whether that be among the highly mainstream Christianity or Islam, or other spiritual traditions, such as Ifá, Voodoo, and Santería. Religion, and spirituality more broadly, offers many people a sense of sanctuary and direction in life, often driven by tenets of compassion, care, and community. However, as humans are fallible and subject to their own egos and shadows, they may also use these belief systems to harm and abuse under the guise of servicing divine order. These harms can be spiritual in nature, such as being shamed for the ways in which you don't adhere to doctrine, or even physical and sexual abuse at the hands of those who use spirituality to mask harm. These harms often go unnamed, creating silence and shame to grow within their victims. Healing from these spiritual abuses begins with the permission to acknowledge and name the harm.

We experience spiritual traditions from an early age. These early years in a religion are important, as they set the foundation for how we see ourselves and make sense of the world around us. We often learn ethics and morality within these teachings, which can make it even more difficult when we find ourselves shamed or harmed by folks in the same tradition.

We lose safety and become confused about our own beliefs, and it can set us off on a course of questioning that is challenging, and in many cases not welcomed by others at all. As a result, we learn to minimize our pain and confusion, especially for the sake of staying connected to family and community.

Many Black men may find themselves with such a history with religion. You may have experienced abuse and mistreatment by parents or caretakers and are still told to honor your mother and father. You may have been told that your gender or sexuality is wrong and that you should be punished for your identity. Even simple acts of natural childhood rebellion may have been met with criticism, shame, and harm, disrupting your connection to a higher power that you saw as benevolent and hopeful. It is profoundly confusing to be told that the one space that was meant to bring you peace in life is also the source of inspiration for your pain and sadness. This reality is hard to reconcile. You may then exist in perpetual confusion about your beliefs, or abandon spirituality altogether as it no longer feels like a safe spiritual home.

If you have been harmed in a place of worship or by a person who claimed to be motivated by holy intentions, know that you are not alone. It does not make you any less of a man to have been subjected to harm or abuse. You did not deserve to experience the harm and shame that you did. Spiritual truth relies on compassion and benevolent action, not shame and fear. I hope you can meet this moment with compassion for the part of you that struggles to connect to your spiritual self because of the harm you've experienced. Whether or not you decide to reconnect or embrace religion or spirituality moving forward is a choice that only you can make. But as you sit in this moment of contemplation and revisit your own experience with spiritual harm, know that acknowledging the truth of your pain is not blasphemous. Your truth is your path to peace. With whom you choose to share your story is your choice alone. Know that whether you choose to share or not, it is your duty to honor your experience and allow yourself to grieve what you have lost. Only then can you begin to reclaim what is spiritually yours.

Your truth is your path to peace.

Release Spiritual Guilt and Own Your Spiritual Journey

When we find ourselves at odds with our spiritual selves, or the religion in which we were raised, we can feel profound guilt for not measuring up to others' expectations. Learning to acknowledge this guilt allows Black men a pathway to find spiritualty that is aligned and meaningful.

MEDITATION: I GIVE MYSELF PERMISSION TO DEFINE SPIRITUALITY ON MY OWN TERMS.

Across the diaspora we have many religious and spiritual traditions. Like members of most families, Black men are often brought up in the norms and customs of their family's traditions and practice its principles from a very young age. As we grow and have our life experiences, we may start to develop our own ideas about spirituality. We develop different relationships with those traditions. At times, these differences in perspective can put us at odds with our family's and culture's spirituality or faith. This can bring about spiritual guilt or shame.

The individual pursuit of spirituality is necessary. Whatever we inherit from family or culture requires a deep personal connection to ensure its continuity within. But this pursuit, due to rigid religious and spiritual programming, can lead others to view this exploration, or distance, as threatening or wrong. This is isolating and can produce a lot of guilt. In these moments you may feel aligned and righteous in your search for meaning, yet may continually face challenges from others because of how you've chosen to navigate spirituality.

Like the many other ideas and perspectives you unconsciously inherit, it is crucial for you to examine the spiritual messages you've internalized. To feel at peace within yourself, you must honor how the messages may, or may not, fit in your life any longer. If you've been navigating this tension and challenge, consider this reflection to be the encouragement to honor your autonomy in your spiritual journey. Guilt is not a helpful motivator in developing and maintaining a relationship with your spiritual beliefs. Freedom and discovery are. As you release guilt and own your spiritual journey, your connection to spirit deepens.

Though you may find tension or discomfort between your beliefs and interpretations from other people in your family and community, guilt is not a pathway forward. Guilt only shames you and keeps you stuck. Black men often face a tremendous amount of influence and pressure to follow community norms or what we may call "honoring the family." This is a noble goal, and yet, for any of us to have a genuine connection to our spiritual selves, we also must make room for self-definition. This is your permission to discover without guilt.

As challenging as it may be, I invite you to give yourself the freedom and permission to discover how spirituality fits into your life, on your own terms. You do not need to be at odds with your family or culture if you choose a different path, nor do you have to hold on to guilt because of your pursuit. Your journey is yours alone.

Access the Sacred Heartbeat

A thumping inside your chest and a life force that sends energy throughout your body, the heartbeat is your sacred connection to spirit, family, and community. In this mindful meditation you will reflect on the powerful relationship between spirit and body with your heartbeat as your guide toward spiritual connection.

MEDITATION: WITH EVERY HEARTBEAT, I AM REMINDED OF MY PLACE AND CONNECTION IN THIS WORLD.

Our lives are often so disconnected these days. We have the most access we have ever had to new ideas and other people, and yet loneliness continues to be one of the top concerns of health officials. Along with social and political divisions, feelings of isolation, loneliness, and depression fester despite our best efforts to log on and be tapped into culture. Why is that? It's because we forget how much we are all connected in the eyes of spirituality.

When we think of what it means to be human and what connects us, something that can go unmentioned is the heart. But each of us has a heart within us that beats. The heart is essential to the body, pushing blood throughout it, delivering oxygen and other nutrients to our systems. It moves waste, like carbon dioxide, out through the lungs.

The heart is also essential to the spirit. It is where we feel warmth when we are cared for. It's where we feel love and connection. The heart is the place that hurts when we lose loved ones and battle grief. The heart is the part of us that threatens to burst when we experience euphoric joy. It is human and spiritual in equal parts, serving both its physiological and spiritual purposes in helping us connect to ourselves and to each other. The heart is sacred.

This meditation offers you a simple exercise. As you sit in this moment in reflection, place one hand on your chest, just over your heart, and take in a deep breath. As you do, remember that no matter what struggles you find yourself navigating in your life, you are never alone. This heartbeat that you feel is the same heartbeat of any brother or sister who is also doing their best to make it through this world. It is a connection to your family, whose genes have helped form this sacred part of you. Your heartbeat is the rhythm that transcends time and place, connecting you with ancestors long gone. This heartbeat is sacred because it connects you to every other human in this world. It is your reminder of all you share with those beings but may not see clearly in your daily life. This heartbeat represents the sacred connection between you and them, and a faith that in this life there is meaning and purpose.

Never forget that this heartbeat is always within you. To connect with yourself, your community, and your spirit, give yourself just a moment to place a hand over your heart, take a breath, and remember that all connection is sacred.

Conclusion

I hope that you found *Mindful Meditations for Black Men* to be a helpful and thoughtful experience. If this is your introduction to the practice of mindfulness, I hope these reflections and meditations have provided respite. If the practice of mindfulness is more familiar to you, I hope you've discovered themes to further integrate into your practice. You've invested in yourself within these pages. Please remember this space, and these entries, are always here for you to develop a more meaningful, compassionate, and intentional relationship with yourself. This book can be the foundation upon which you continue to build, honor, and empower yourself.

The world that we find ourselves in right now is challenging, but not without opportunity for more inner peace. In the United States in particular, we're dealing with the rise of authoritarianism, racism, anti-Semitism, homophobia, and transphobia. It is a difficult time to be a human. With the rising cost of living, incredible barriers to home ownership, and the pressures that we face daily to live our lives as our best selves, things can feel overwhelming at times. Fortunately, when you give yourself the power of presence in mindfulness, you practice healing and resilience in real time.

Mindfulness is not a solution to these societal ills. Mindfulness is a tool to help you find moments of refuge and learn to exist with perspectives that help you embrace more compassion for yourself and the world around you. No one exists in isolation. You are a member of a larger community. And as you take better care of yourself, you become a better community member too. When you devote the time to invest in yourself and heal parts of yourself that need healing, you give yourself the opportunity to show up as a more mindful and nurturing part of the larger community. Mindfulness enables you to do just these things.

In moments of uncertainty, you need tools and resources that help you maintain a sense of grounding and intentionality in your life. These tools also enable you to create space for moments of joy. After all, joy is resistance. Pride is resistance. Cultural connection and brotherhood are resistance. Revisit the passages in this book to remind yourself of what is most important to you and connect to these moments of healing, inner peace, and joy.

As you continue to evolve on your journey of mindfulness and thoughtful living, I hope that you also share what you've learned and the experiences that you've felt with other Black men around you. Live boldly with self-awareness and mindfulness as gifts that you can share and embody alongside your community. Strengthened by these principles, you will experience more health and peace as you not only survive but thrive with each step forward in life. You may also inspire others to do the same.

Additional Resources

Developing a spiritual practice is a highly personalized and unique process. After spending time with *Mindful Meditations for Black Men* you may have some interest in additional resources that will help you on your journey. In this section, you'll find some books, card decks, and websites related to the topics of mindfulness and spirituality. These tools will further help you develop a deeper and healthier relationship with yourself. Keep in mind that not every resource works for everyone. I invite you to see these resources as inspiration for cultivating your own unique spiritual practice.

Books

Patriarchy Blues: Reflections on Manhood by Frederick Joseph. Written by *New York Times* bestselling author Frederick Joseph, *Patriarchy Blues* offers a perspective rather than a roadmap on discovering masculinity that's expansive and rooted in more compassion, both for self and community, all from a Black man's perspective.

Peace Is Every Step: The Path of Mindfulness in Everyday Life by Thich Nhat Hanh. Hanh was a leader in meditation and mindfulness and made his home in France's Plum Village, where he taught on the principles of Buddhism and present-centered living until his passing in 2022. This title is a great resource in learning to embrace mindfulness as a way of life.

Post Traumatic Slave Syndrome: America's Legacy of Enduring Injury and Healing by Dr. Joy DeGruy. This book is one of the most important volumes in Black mental health. Scholar Dr. DeGruy compiles over a decade of research to offer insights into the Black experience and the impact of slavery on folks across the African Diaspora.

The Power of Now: A Guide to Spiritual Enlightenment by Eckhart Tolle. This was the book that introduced me to the concept of mindfulness and present-centered living. Originally published in 1997, it remains one of the most important texts in recent decades on mindfulness and spirituality.

The Will to Change: Men, Masculinity, and Love by bell hooks. This book offers incredible insight into the challenges men face in discovering healthy masculinity. As most works by hooks, it is in equal parts informative and confronting. This resource will help you take a closer look at your experiences with gender and masculinity and invite deep personal exploration.

Card Decks

Compassion Cards by Pema Chödrön. In this deck, world-renowned Buddhist monk and teacher Pema Chödrön offers insight into the practice of *lojong*, which helps train the mind and heart through daily contemplation. Each card offers insight into a tenet of *lojong* and features commentary from Chödrön to apply it to everyday life.
https://pemachodronfoundation.org/product/compassion-cards/

Gratitude Blooming Reflection Card Deck by Gratitude Blooming. Gratitude is a helpful gateway to enhancing spirituality and better mental health. This card deck from Gratitude Blooming is a great resource to do a quick card pull and reflect on the themes on the card for spiritual connection and inspiration for the day or week ahead.

https://shop.gratitudeblooming.com/collections/shop/products/gratitude-blooming-card-deck

The Shadow Work Self-Reflection Deck by Jor-El Caraballo. This deck is adapted from my first book, *The Shadow Work Workbook: Self-Care Exercises for Healing Your Trauma and Exploring Your Hidden Self.* This deck offers 100 prompts for self-reflection to help you access the often-hidden parts of psyche that aren't consciously explored in daily life.
www.simonandschuster.com/books/The-Shadow-Work-Self-Reflection-Deck/Jor-El-Caraballo/9781507224281

Websites and Platforms

Black Boys Om. A grassroots organization dedicated to promoting health and wellness for Black men and boys. The organization hosts mind-body workshops and retreats. They also help train Black men to become wellness practitioners, and they host a Registered Yoga Teacher (RYT) training program.
https://blackboysom.org

Express Yourself Black Man. A website, a provider directory resource, and an online platform created by and for Black men. Their website and social media content regularly promote mental health and wellness content, empowering Black men with the perspectives and resources to live healthier lives.
www.expressyourselfblackman.com

Native Son. Founded by journalist Emil Wilbekin, Native Son promotes the health and well-being of Black gay and Queer men. Through their forums, online platform, and annual Native Son Awards, the

organization advocates and celebrates the contributions of Black gay and Queer men in society.
https://nativeson.us

Spirituality & Health. A magazine that helps promote a variety of spiritual principles and modalities in their monthly publication. This is a great resource to explore a variety of spiritual ideas, themes, and spiritual wellness practitioners.
www.spiritualityhealth.com

Index

About the Author

Jor-El Caraballo, LMHC, is a licensed therapist and cofounder of Viva, a multistate mental health practice. Caraballo received a BA in psychology from the University of North Carolina at Wilmington, and MA and EdM degrees in psychological counseling from Teachers College, Columbia University. He has been featured as a mental health expert across many magazines and websites, including *mindbodygreen*, *Men's Health*, *Healthline*, *Insider*, *Self*, and more, sharing advice and insight on self-care, interpersonal relationships, dealing with trauma, and more.